The 100 Greatest

Entertainment WEEKLY

Greatest

Enter
tain
ers

1950

2000

Contents

the Countdown

Imagine a world without *Thriller, Jaws,* or "D'oh!" Life would go on, of course—but it wouldn't have a beat you could dance to. Herewith, 1 to 100, those who kept us entertained, and not just weekly, either.

1   The Beatles
2   Elvis Presley
3   Marilyn Monroe
4   Steven Spielberg
5   Madonna
6   Frank Sinatra
7   *Saturday Night Live*
8   Michael Jackson
9   Lucille Ball
10 *The Simpsons*
11 Bob Dylan
12 Marlon Brando
13 Barbra Streisand
14 Alfred Hitchcock
15 The Rolling Stones
16 Audrey Hepburn
17 John Wayne
18 Elizabeth Taylor
19 Aretha Franklin
20 Robert De Niro
21 Stephen King
22 Mary Tyler Moore
23 Jack Nicholson

24 Bill Cosby
25 Robert Redford
26 Woody Allen
27 Clint Eastwood
28 Tom Wolfe
29 Stevie Wonder
30 Martin Scorsese
31 Oprah Winfrey
32 Paul Newman
33 *Star Trek*
34 Richard Pryor
35 Bruce Springsteen
36 James Brown
37 Harrison Ford
38 Meryl Streep
39 Miles Davis
40 Norman Lear
41 James Dean

42 Francis Ford Coppola
43 Tom Hanks
44 Bob Marley
45 Johnny Carson
46 James L. Brooks

47 Jackie Gleason
48 Jane Fonda
49 Julia Roberts
50 Chuck Berry
51 Jimi Hendrix
52 Tom Cruise
53 Dustin Hoffman
54 David Bowie
55 The Beach Boys
56 Jerry Seinfeld
57 Stanley Kubrick
58 Cher
59 Prince
60 Willie Nelson
61 Jim Henson
62 Warren Beatty
63 Jodie Foster
64 Joni Mitchell
65 David Letterman
66 Jim Carrey
67 Aaron Spelling
68 Ed Sullivan
69 The Sex Pistols
70 Paul Simon
71 Steve Martin
72 Kurt Cobain
73 Neil Young

74 Michael Crichton
75 *The X-Files*
76 Run DMC
77 Monty Python
78 Bob Newhart
79 Diana Ross
80 Michael Jordan
81 Agnes Nixon
82 Eric Clapton
83 John Grisham
84 Sean Connery
85 Carol Burnett
86 Mel Brooks
87 Steven Bochco
88 Loretta Lynn
89 Janis Joplin

90 The Grateful Dead
91 Robin Williams
92 Oliver Stone
93 Bob Fosse
94 Elvis Costello
95 James Cameron
96 Diane Keaton
97 James Garner
98 Garth Brooks
99 Spike Lee
100 Chrissie Hynde

the Maste

Quick, what do Aretha Franklin, Marlon Brando, Richard Pryor, John Wayne, Martin Scorsese, Kurt Cobain, and Oprah Winfrey have in common? ✦ The short answer: They're all people for whom the word *entertainer* doesn't begin to do justice. ✦ *One Hundred Greatest Sui Generis Pop Colossi* doesn't really leap off a book cover, though, does it? But that's what the folks above are—not to mention the dozens of their peers from the past half century whom we're celebrating in this *100 Greatest Entertainers* book. For lack of a defining term, let's just call *them* defining—of the media and of the art forms in which they've worked, of the times in which they've lived, and of the culture that would look oddly empty without them. ✦ We chose to focus on the century's second half, not because we have anything against D.W. Griffith, but because the modern pop-cult era truly got started after World War II, with the arrival of television, rock & roll, and an itchy, omnivorous youth audience. That mix has created figures who've changed the way we see the world—Elvis and Madonna, Kubrick and Spielberg, Mary Tyler Moore and the cast of

rClass

Saturday Night Live. But also making their mark have been behind-the-scenes creators like Norman Lear, ahead-of-their-time groundbreakers like James Brown, unstinting artists like Joni Mitchell, and those who've just entertained so well that they've put their stamp on an era (everyone from Jackie Gleason to Julia Roberts). You'll also find a section on key influences from around the world. As for ranking our 100 Greatest—sure, it may ultimately be silly to compare, say, the Beatles with Meryl Streep. But there is a certain calculus of pop impact, artistic legacy, entertainment value, and (okay) sheer gut instinct behind our chutzpah. ✦ In short, these are the people we feel our great-grandchildren will still recognize in 2099, in the same way we know the names Sarah Bernhardt, Mark Twain, and Enrico Caruso. By then, perhaps, ENTERTAINMENT WEEKLY'S *The Greatest Entertainers of the 21st Century* will be downloaded directly into readers' frontal lobes. But *Rear Window,* "Do Right Woman—Do Right Man," the Killer Bees Sketch, and *The Bonfire of the Vanities* will still be hitting them where they live. —TY BURR

1

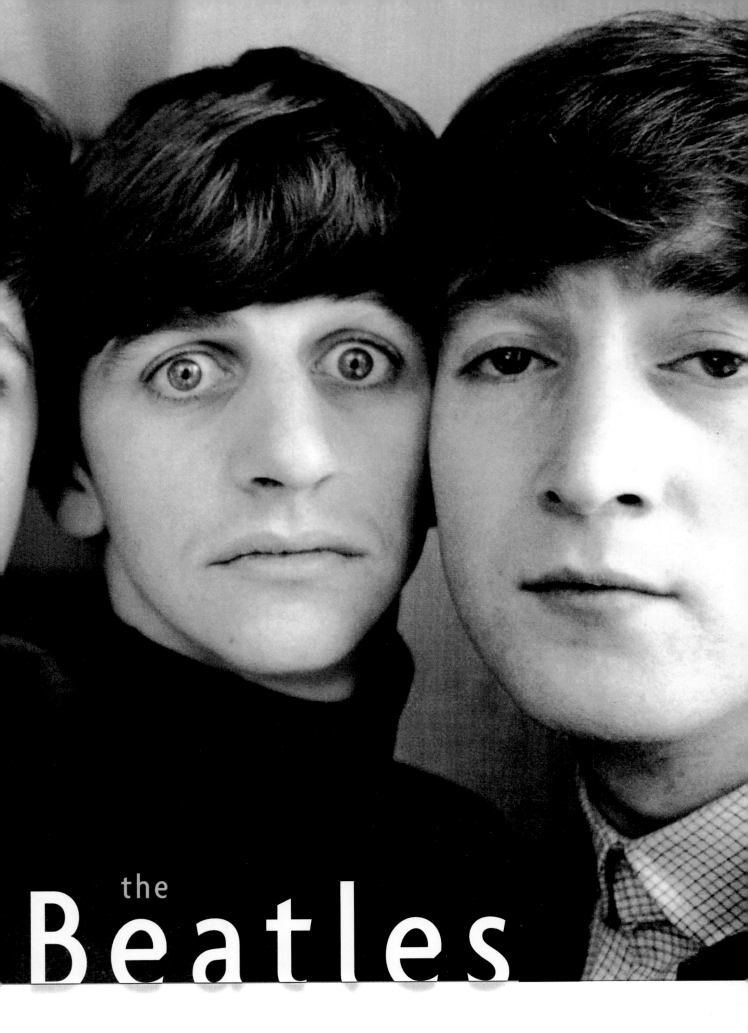

the Beatles

THE AIRPORT HAD A NEW NAME: JOHN F. KENNEDY. ✦ JUST THREE months earlier, the President of the United States had been shot and killed. And so, in the city of New York, the powers that be had rechristened the airport in his honor. This made sense, in some weird karmic way: If President Kennedy had symbolized a generation's aching hunger for vitality and beauty and the thrill of *newness*, well, so did the airport. It was postwar America's Ellis Island, the glass-and-chromium portal through which global seekers caught their first glimpse of a new world.

On this particular day—Feb. 7, 1964—four seekers from the Old World were preparing to pass through customs. They landed at John F. Kennedy International Airport on a Pan Am jet called the *Clipper Defiance*. Which also made a lot of sense: Zany and jubilant, their arrival would defy the gloom that had enveloped the United States all winter.

Radio stations were trumpeting their arrival as if demigods were descending from Mount Olympus; thousands of kids were showing up to greet them with howls and shrieks. Intrigued, an enterprising young reporter from *The New York Herald-Tribune* cruised out to the airport to see what all the fuss was about.

"I was there at Kennedy Airport when the Beatles arrived," Tom Wolfe remembers. "I'll never forget the sight of hundreds of boys, high school students, running down a hallway at the international arrivals building with their combs out, converting their duck-tail hairdos into bangs. They'd just seen the Beatles. They were packed on this balcony watching the Beatles arrive. They saw these haircuts, and they started combing their hair forward so it would fall over their foreheads like the Beatles. I never will forget that scene. That was symbolic of a big change; the last semblance of adult control of music *vanished* at that moment."

From the vantage point of popular culture, you'd be hard-pressed to find a day more flushed and fervid with the prospect of change, a moment more electric with mondo-seismic *shift*, than Feb. 7, 1964. At the precise instant those American kids whipped out their combs, a global metamorphosis ratcheted into high gear. It spread. Fast. It would tear across the landscape like a brushfire.

First, there was that famous press conference. Winking at the media madness that would eventually swallow the century, the Beatles spent their first few minutes in the New World fielding goofball questions from the Manhattan scoop patrol. What people saw from this publicity contrivance was important: four grinning lads in matching suits with these shockingly symmetrical, draped-down-to-the-eyebrows haircuts. But what people heard was way more profound.

A reporter: "Will you sing something for us?"

John Lennon: "We need money first."

We need money first. That didn't sound like something Elvis Presley would ever say. Those four simple words—"We need money first"—quaked with a whole new mutant strain of celebrity energy. They were delivered in a liquidy Liverpudlian brogue; they were funny, sarcastic, brash, self-deprecating, and true—all at the same time. Clearly, John Lennon, a man who would become a pop-culture martyr one day, was not going to use this moment in the spotlight to bow and scrape and profess his undying adoration for his mum. No, the press would take its cue from him.

A reporter: "Was your family in show business?"

John Lennon: "Well, me dad used to say me mother was a great performer."

Elvis would *never* say that.

This was just the beginning. Already gargantuan in their homeland, the Beatles had come to America to cross the Rubicon; the high-pitched hysteria of Feb. 7 wound up being a mere prelude to a cataclysm. Two days after their arrival at Kennedy Airport, the Beatles performed on *The Ed Sullivan Show*.

Seventy-three million people watched—at the time, the biggest audience in TV history. One was a 13-year-old boy whose name upon birth in Israel was Chaim Witz. Years later, as Gene Simmons, he would breathe fire and spit blood and play bass in a band called Kiss. "When the Beatles first appeared on *The Ed Sullivan Show*, it was probably one of the milestones in human history," Simmons says now. "There are what scientists call singularities. They happen every once in a while and have a quantum effect on life as we know it on the face of the planet. When the Beatles first appeared, it really changed the world.

"I remember watching," he goes on. "It was as poignant a moment as when the monolith appeared in front of those apes in *2001*. It changed my sense of being. I mean, it was close to a religious experience. I remember watching it and initially thinking, Oh, they look kind of silly. To *myself*. But when my mother came in and put the food on the table, I remember her comment was 'Oh, they look silly.'

"At that point I realized that they were cool. Because as long as my mother thought they were silly, of course I'd have to think they were cool."

IF ALL THE BEATLES EVER DID WAS WHIP UP A TEEN FROTH IN THE early 1960s, they'd still rank among the most amazing acts of the century. Beatlemania, after all, has become the gold standard against which all youthquakes are measured, whether the source of the tremor is Michael Jackson or Leonardo DiCaprio. But what the

SIMPLY THE BEST

MEET THE BEATLES (1964)
The sound of a stoked, shrieking youthquake in full bloom. Featuring: "I Want to Hold Your Hand" and "All My Loving."

RUBBER SOUL (1965)
Forever the sweet quintessence of British folk-pop. Featuring: "Norwegian Wood," "In My Life," and "Drive My Car."

IN THEIR LIFE (1) Fans in London get ready to swoon; (2) the Fab Four with Ed Sullivan during a rehearsal for the group's first appearance on his variety show in 1964; (3) ...with love, John Lennon signs autographs in England in 1963.

Beatles accomplished before, after, and in spite of the gale-force squeals—that's what qualifies John Lennon, Paul McCartney, George Harrison, and Ringo Starr as the greatest entertainers of our time.

Hell, the Beatles deserve to top the list purely for the creation of "A Day in the Life," the billowing climax of *Sgt. Pepper's Lonely Hearts Club Band*, a song that seems to carry all the sadness and tumult and folly of the 20th century in the gentle limbs of its melody. They deserve to conquer the list for that morning in 1964 when Paul McCartney rolled out of bed at the George V Hotel in Paris, plopped down at a piano, and wove the cobwebs of a dream into "Yesterday," a ballad that according to folklore would later be recorded by more singers than any tune in the history of popular music. They deserve to rule the list for getting away with lyrics as simple as "All you need is love" and "We can work it out" and "Let it be," and for getting away with lyrics as psychotropically convoluted as "Semolina Pilchard climbing up the Eiffel Tower" and "Picture yourself in a boat on a river with tangerine trees and marmalade skies" and "He got monkey finger, he shoot Coca-Cola."

"The obtuse, stream-of-consciousness lyrics that I write definitely come from the John Lennon stuff, especially around the White Album," says Robert Pollard, leader of the Fab Four-drenched indie band Guided by Voices. "Stuff that doesn't make any sense—

REVOLVER (1966)
Leaving puppy love behind, the Beatles grope toward psychedelia and chamber-pop with "Tomorrow Never Knows" and "Eleanor Rigby."

THE BEATLES (1968)
"Helter Skelter" is right: This behemoth is a messy, sprawling, sweet-and-sour document of a band on the brink. Better known as the White Album, it also features "Blackbird," "Back in the U.S.S.R.," and "Ob-La-Di, Ob-La-Da."

ABBEY ROAD (1969)
Before the split heard round the world, the Beatles achieved a state of grace with a record as twinkly and delicate as a crystal chandelier.

just complete gibberish—is always more interesting."

Still, you won't catch a whiff of such radical experiments in early Merseybeat documents like *Please Please Me* and *With the Beatles*. The Fab Four started out as little more than an adrenalized frat-party band, roasting R&B chestnuts in some of the most putrid sweatboxes in England and Germany. Their scorching covers of other people's songs ("Twist and Shout," "Roll Over Beethoven," "Boys," "Dizzy Miss Lizzie") nearly eclipsed their own. But not for long.

Quickly, they began to crank out hits. Impeccable hits. "I Want to Hold Your Hand," "She Loves You," "Can't Buy Me Love," "Ticket to Ride," "Day Tripper," "Hello Goodbye," "Something," "Here Comes the Sun," "Help!" They wrote songs for children, loony jingles that seemed to swing on some spectral circus trapeze: "Maxwell's Silver Hammer," "Rocky Raccoon," "Being for the Benefit of Mr. Kite!" They wrote songs to scare children—songs surging with the fires of hell: "Helter Skelter," "Revolution 9," "Happiness Is a Warm Gun." They composed ballads that can still make you weep like a child every time you come across them: "In My Life," "Blackbird," "If I Fell," "Hey Jude," "For No One," "She's Leaving Home," "Julia."

The Beatles grew too big for the century that bore them: *Revolver*, a creative turning point in 1966, seems to catapult through time itself, whirling from a 17th-century chamber suite ("Eleanor Rigby") to a 19th-century sea chantey ("Yellow Submarine") to a 21st-century cyclone of cosmic musings, freak feedback, and rhythmic hypnosis ("Tomorrow Never Knows").

It's this legacy, this mountain of work, that stands as sturdy and mythic as Westminster Abbey. Even after the shameless Nike commercials that used "Revolution" to hawk rubber soles. Even after "Free as a Bird" and "Real Love," two drippy mediocrities that Paul, George, and Ringo tried to claim were "new" Beatles songs amid the *Anthology* hype of 1995. Even after Linda McCartney's curious embellishment of "Hey Jude." Even after the Broadway musical. "Let's be honest here," says Simmons. "I couldn't shine Lennon and McCartney's boots. I couldn't shine George Harrison's boots when it comes to songwriting. They're clearly the most popular songwriters of all time. That's bigger than Gershwin, bigger than all of 'em."

"Every band, even when they don't want to admit it, has to be somewhat influenced by the Beatles," says Pollard. "There are some people who have a kind of anti-Beatles stance, but I just can't imagine that. Most people acknowledge that the Beatles were the greatest band of all time."

A REPORTER IN 1964: "JOHN, IS IT A FAD?" ✦ JOHN LENNON: "OBVIously. Anything in this business is a fad. We don't think we're going to last forever. We're just going to have a good time while it lasts."

For once, the guy was wrong.

Between July 6, 1957 (when John and Paul first scoped each other out at the St. Peter's Parish Church Garden Fete in a Liverpool suburb), and April 10, 1970 (when Paul announced that he'd quit the band), the Beatles did the following: Sold over 100 million albums. Scored 20 No. 1 singles. Persuaded millions of kids to pick up electric guitars. Formed an alliance with brilliant and buttoned-up producer George Martin, the prophet who advised them to "think symphonically." Captured the essence of joy on celluloid with *A Hard Day's Night*. Experimented with drugs. Offended the church. Inspired people to burn vinyl in bonfires. Stopped going on stage—at the crest of their fame—in order to cloister themselves in the fertile womb of *Abbey Road*. Grew beards. Went in search of spiritual enlightenment in Indian ashrams. Pioneered the notion of "music video." Paved the way for Saturday morning's shimmy-pop cartoons with an animated movie, *Yellow Submarine*. Established the concept of rock-as-art with *Sgt. Pepper's Lonely Hearts Club Band* and the White Album and *Abbey Road*. Flirted with various modes of revolutionary thought. Captured the essence of frustration on celluloid with *Let It Be*.

Then they broke up, leaving a scar on the face of the world. (Our consolation: magnificent solo albums like George's *All Things Must Pass*, Paul's *Band on the Run*, and John's *Imagine*.)

"It was spiritual music," Simmons muses. "It was a gentle prodding to open up your eyes. They weren't heavy-handed about it. They didn't lead you. They put a spotlight on a point of view. I mean, if they had run for Kings of the World, I'm sure they would've been voted in. Lennon was really right, you know—about being more popular than Christ. No question about it. It was a new way of thinking, that's what it was. When you heard the Beatles, it was not the language of your mom and dad. It was clear, it was clean, like a breath of fresh air. They said the same things that Mom and Dad said, because Mom and Dad said, 'I love you.' The Beatles used the same words, but somehow in different ways. It just sounded true. What it sounded like was 'That's from the heart.'"

Beyond the music, though, the Beatles deserve to dominate this list because they serve as a Rosetta stone for your own identity. They force you to *choose*. If you grew up in the latter half of the 20th century, at some point you came to a fateful fork in the road; you had to proclaim your allegiance to John, Paul, George, or Ringo. You knew what their first names stood for, at least the stereotypes. John: the firebrand, the caustic Socrates, the guy who always answered by firing back a question or a pun or a scalding quip.

A reporter in 1965: "How do you feel about teenagers imitating you with Beatle wigs?"

John Lennon: "They're not imitating us because we don't wear Beatle wigs."

Paul: the Cute Beatle, the doe-eyed softy and master melodist, the lover of sheepdogs and Penny Lane and vaudeville ditties. ("But the truth is, it was McCartney who was much more the edgy art guy," Simmons offers as a corrective. "The pop guy who likes cornflakes and wears sweaters? Wrong.") George: cool and quiet and distant and inward, prone to Eastern mysticism and apt to wheel a sitar into the studio. Ringo: the jester, the reality check, the bloke with the big schnozz and the "How the hell did I get so lucky?" grin on his face.

One way or another, they were *us*.

HOW FAR DID THE BEATLES go? And how far did we go with them? ✦ Here's a picture: The date is Jan. 30, 1969, almost five years to the day since the Fab Four—beaming with those big smiles and dark *Reservoir Dogs* suits and that Wildean moptop wit—touched down at John F. Kennedy International Airport for the first time. *Only five years*, and yet a chasm has been crossed.

Now sporting stringy Nazarene hair and Wild West muttonchops and baggy eyes and mismatched clothes that might've been plucked from the two-shilling bin at the Haight-Ashbury Goodwill,

GOOD DAY, SUNSHINE The band is all smiles in the church garden of London's St. Pancras in 1968

the Beatles look washed-out and bedraggled. They look grown-up. They look...*spent*. Which is precisely how they feel.

On Jan. 30, 1969, the Beatles and John's joined-at-the-hip soul mate, Yoko Ono, are crawling toward the climax of the notorious *Let It Be* sessions. For four harrowing weeks, they've been fighting against fragmentation, torpor, and each other. If they came off like cuddly quadruplets on *The Ed Sullivan Show*, well, "by the time *Let It Be* happened they were four very different men," says Michael Lindsay-Hogg, who directed the documentary film about the making of that album. "And they just wanted something else."

Just 20 days earlier, in fact, George Harrison had quit the band in disgust. His departure was followed by a session of primal screaming that's never been played for the public, even though Lindsay-Hogg caught it on film. "When George left the group, the other ones went back down into the studio and they started to play this really demonic riff," he recalls. "And then Yoko sat on George's blue pillow, and she sang her kind of crazy caterwauling singing, and they played for like half an hour. I mean, just *desperate* music. Desperate, desperate. They had this outburst of anger—anger at him leaving, anger at their needing him, anger at maybe where they'd gotten to."

George came back, eventually. Nevertheless the Beatles were exhausted and edgy on Jan. 30. *Let It Be*'s film crew needed a spry

coda for their documentary—"something kind of oomphy to go out on," Lindsay-Hogg says—so they wanted the Beatles to climb to the roof of Apple Studios, plug in their amps, and strafe the stuffy London precinct of Saville Row with their first live blast of rock & roll since 1966. "Typical of the Beatles, we were supposed to go up on the roof at 12:30, and they were still arguing at 12:25 about *if* they would do it at all," the director remembers. "Of course, I was tearing my hair out, because I knew there was something up there—there was something golden on the roof."

Then suddenly they said yes. Lennon smirked at his band mates. "Oh, fook it," he said. "Let's do it." They walked up a narrow staircase and opened a door to the roof. Under a sky the color of milky Earl Grey, surrounded by steeples and chimney pots, the Beatles played for a small, bemused audience—a crowd not unlike those they used to encounter in Liverpool and Hamburg.

They had a couple of tender songs in their new repertoire—tearjerkers like "Let It Be" and "The Long and Winding Road," both of which sounded like omens of their own demise. But they didn't play those songs on the roof. As bankers and tailors and secretaries and old ladies—characters straight out of "Penny Lane" or "Eleanor Rigby"—gazed up from the street in confusion, the Beatles launched into the solar-baked boogie of "Get Back." The stripped-to-the-bone blues of "Don't Let Me Down." The lung-busting gospel purgation of "I've Got a Feeling." And "One After 909," a long-lost rockabilly rave-up that Lennon had written when he was 17.

They grinned at one another. They laughed. "This lovely thing happened. They *enjoyed* it," Lindsay-Hogg remembers. "It was like they were 17 again. The last time was like the first time. Which doesn't always happen in life."

And at the end of this, the Beatles' final performance, just as London cops were marching to the roof to shut it down, John Lennon leaned into the mike and cracked a joke. "I'd like to say thank you on behalf of the group," he said, "and I hope we passed the audition." —JEFF GORDINIER

elvis Presley

"I'LL TELL YOU WHAT IT WAS: ELVIS PUT SOME grease in rock & roll—some cooking grease, music like bacon drippin's," says the funk-music guru George Clinton. "He was as funky as a white boy could be, and that freaked out some people, and made a lot more people love him." ✦ Clinton is right on the money, and still has only half the story. For when it comes to Elvis Presley, contradictions and paradoxes abound. It is fair to say that no single figure in American popular culture has meant so many different things to so many people as Elvis Presley did, and in not a few instances continues to do so. To some, Presley is the ultimate Horatio Alger story, the embodiment of a dirt-poor youth who pulled himself up by his bootstraps to achieve monumental success. To others, he is rock music's chameleon genius, the creator of convincing recordings of everything from raucous rockabilly to fervent gospel to faux–Italian opera like "It's Now or Never." ✦ And to a different group of people, Presley will always remain the beginning of the end of decent, respectable culture—the untutored pop star whose achievement was a sham, a scandal. You know the accusations: Others wrote his material; he stole his style from black performers; he bad-mouthed hippies and begged President Nixon to certify him a federal narcotics agent even while descending into a decadent lifestyle of drugs and (shudder) fried peanut-butter-and-banana sandwiches. Certainly his self-suffocating fame—a stardom that ended up cutting him off from his worldwide audience, leaving him in a limbo of enabling cronies and a wack drug habit—also serves as rock's ultimate cautionary tale. ✦ But before the tragedy there was the triumph, the emergence in the mid-'50s of the Folk Music Fireball, as Presley was nicknamed in those days, inciter of wild teen adulation. As George Clinton notes: "They didn't even call it rock & roll when he was starting out. People still called it 'pop' music. Powder-dry, Pat Boone, pop music. Elvis didn't care about that; he zeroed in on rhythm & blues, country, and gospel. Elvis could sing the blues, but what he really knew

KING'S HANDSOME (1) Presley, ready for his closeup in 1956 on *The Ed Sullivan Show*; (2) fans hope to turn the King into the Prez; (3) 1957's *Jailhouse Rock* is considered his finest film; (4) in 1958 he's in the army now; (5) glad handing in Mississippi in 1956

was rhythm—he knew there was rhythm in the church, singing gospel, and rhythm in country music, the way Hank Williams sang it. Elvis put it all together and slathered it with that low-down, sexy greasiness, wigglin' on stage like he was almost slippin' on this grease he was giving out. That's what made the little girls go crazy."

Few of the 98 entertainers who follow came from a more impoverished, culturally deprived, sociologically hopeless background. Yet Presley, for all his gaudy bad taste (in clothes, in furniture, in food), was an aesthete as an artist, with remarkably informed, varied taste in choosing the country, gospel, and R&B songs he wanted to cover and make his own. The Beatles, by dint of their four-man synthesis of originality and fresh ideas, disseminated more revolutionary ideas and had a more eclectic sound. But the Fab Four readily acknowledged the unprecedented new freedom that Presley's music represented. Thus John Lennon's famous quote: "Before Elvis, there was nothing."

Something, therefore—something downright uncanny—was loosed upon the world on Jan. 8, 1935, when twin boys, Elvis Aron and the stillborn Jesse Garon, were delivered by a doctor in the ramshackle home of parents Vernon and Gladys Presley. Raised in a poor neighborhood in Tupelo, Miss., Elvis—the son of a fitful-

ly hardworking man who'd done jail time for check fraud while his son was still a baby—might easily have remained the working-class laborer his milieu decreed he was destined to be (in Elvis' specific case, a truck driver, a job he continued to hold even after he began making his first recordings, with Sun Records).

Instead, he formed alliances, first with Sun's owner-producer, Sam Phillips, and then with manager Colonel Tom Parker, both of whom recognized that Presley's best performances compressed the full-force gale of his personality in two- or three-minute bursts. In the time it took for a single like "Good Rockin' Tonight" or "Don't Be Cruel" or "Stuck on You" or "Return to Sender" or "Burning Love" to be heard, you understood the unique combination of sexual bravado, emotional sensitivity, and disciplined musicality that lay behind the singing. Like the crooners he admired—Dean Martin, Bing Crosby—Presley made it all seem as natural as breathing. Yet his central artistic paradox is that he worked hard to achieve effortlessness, which is also the quality that made him stand out among frenetic rock & roll peers like Little Richard and Jerry Lee Lewis.

Presley and Parker knew that paradox could be translated into the movies. With a few exceptions, however, the films Parker chose were schlock. Presley could overcome junk in the recording

studio, where he insisted on endless retakes until he could turn often-mediocre songs into worthwhile music, but he could not overcome the layers of producers, directors, and screenwriters who oversaw his movies. As a result, Presley remains a great entertainer only in the recording studio and on stage. The recent second volume of Peter Guralnick's definitive biography, *Careless Love: The Unmaking of Elvis Presley*, chronicles the ways in which his extra-musical indulgences in drugs, in a celebrity that exhausted him, and in simple laziness finally combined to defeat him. But none of the sad, lurid stories from Presley detract from the lasting excitement and endless revelations of his music, or of taped performances such as his 1968 NBC comeback special.

It's no wonder some people believe Presley survived his fatal drug overdose of Aug. 16, 1977. In any given week, it is virtually impossible to avoid an encounter with the King. One day, I'm listening to hip-hop madman Kool Keith's latest CD, *Black Elvis/ Lost in Space*, while reading a book of poems by Robert Polito, and I come across the lines "Nights we commune with our fat cat/Elvis, black genius of the new…" Weird coincidence? Not at all. Last August, a contestant on ABC's *Who Wants to Be a Millionaire*—a math teacher, mind you—wore an Elvis necktie for good luck. (The sartorial decision was so blithe, so casual, so commonplace,

host Regis Philbin didn't even comment on it.) Soon after, *The New York Times* reported that the English rock singer and guitarist Kevin Coyne is readying a Presley musical tentatively titled *Fat Old Hero*. Fat, thin; young, old: Elvis Presley is, in the words of Mojo Nixon's dumb but nevertheless true 1987 song, "everywhere."

But why? It's rare now to hear Elvis' music except on oldies stations. And his movies are rarely watched for anything other than laughs. Why the lingering presence? Atmosphere. Like Marilyn Monroe, his female equivalent in iconographic terms, Elvis summoned up more than music, more than stardom. He contained paradoxical attitudes peculiar to America: part rebel, part nostalgist; part sex-crazy, part aw-shucks innocent; part sneer and wiggle, part yearning and pleading. So though he burst onto the scene entirely new, transforming attitudes and behavior, he was blank enough to become a screen, someone to project our own desires upon. That he died young made this all the easier.

Pop culture works not only in mysterious but pervasive ways. Presley changed us; we, in our continuing remembrance of him, continue to change him. It's this symbiotic relationship between performer and audience that guarantees Elvis will never really "leave the building." —KEN TUCKER

marilyn
Monroe

TO NORMAN MAILER, WHO WROTE A BOOK ABOUT her, she was a "castrator-queen." To Gloria Steinem, who wrote a book about her, she was "vulnerable and unprotected." To Elton John, who sang a song about her, she was a "candle in the wind." To every woman according to her abilities, to every man according to his needs, in life and in death, Marilyn Monroe was something more than just the facts. ✦ The former Norma Jeane Baker, who had lived in an orphanage, was an actress, yes. She traded her head of average brown curls for blond-bombshell status, true. She was a walking confection of sexuality, a lonely and insecure little girl, an object of desire for the man in the street and the President in the White House. And when she died in 1962 of a drug overdose, at the age of 36, her acting teacher, Lee Strasberg, tried to describe her aura in a eulogy: "She had a luminous quality," he said, "a combination of wistfulness, radiance, yearning...to set her apart, and yet it made everyone wish to be part of it, to share in the childish

naïveté which was at once so shy and yet so vibrant." ✦ Strasberg might also have mentioned Monroe's estimable comic abilities—the work of a woman who knew exactly what kind of commotion she could cause, and guilelessly enjoyed the effect. (She got the joke that sex can turn men into mice.) As the forthright fortune hunter Lorelei Lee in *Gentlemen Prefer Blondes*, slaying gents with a glance, and especially as the one and only Sugar Kane in *Some Like It Hot*, the actress who knew how to play dumb proved that she was anything but. She proved, too, that she could be catnip to women as well as to men, since moviegoing gals have got to love the moxie of any siren so amused by the power of her own va-va-voomness. ✦ And Strasberg might also have pointed out the very different effect Monroe achieved in her serious dramas—knocking the boots off hornswoggled cowboy Don Murray in *Bus Stop* or tying Clark Gable in knots in her last film, *The Misfits* (written by husband No. 3, Arthur Miller). As effervescently as she could

3

PHOTOGRAPH BY PHILIPPE HALSMAN

SIMPLY THE BEST

ALL ABOUT EVE (1950)
One of Monroe's earliest performances is also one of her earliest essence–of–"Dumb Blond (or Is She?)" roles as a graduate of the "Copacabana School of Dramatic Arts."

GENTLEMEN PREFER BLONDES (1953)
In which she sang "Diamonds Are a Girl's Best Friend" in the voice of a little girl but with the wisdom of a smart, funny woman.

BUS STOP (1956)
If there were any doubts that the blond could actually *act*, they were erased by her sure portrayal of a saloon singer.

▲ *SOME LIKE IT HOT* (1959)
Monroe worked at the height of her funny-sexbomb powers opposite Jack Lemmon and Tony Curtis in drag.

"HAPPY BIRTHDAY, MR. PRESIDENT" (1962)
Modern politics and happening Hollywood make whoopee. At a party for JFK Monroe whisper-sang in a whisper-size dress.

play comedy, Monroe embodied victimhood, imbuing her characters with poignant believability. She demonstrated an amazingly flexible theatrical range (enough to attract *Prince and the Showgirl* director and costar Sir Laurence Olivier, for Pete's sake) and underappreciated career savvy.

Thirty-seven years after her death, new facts are still being assembled about the woman, the people with whom she was intimate, and the circumstances of her death, adding to an already extensive library of books, movies, and TV projects. "Never before seen" photographs are still being offered of one of the most photogenic performers of the 20th century. (If possible, Monroe was even more dynamic a presence in still photos than in moving pictures.) And her brief marriage to baseball great Joe DiMaggio still ranks as one of the 20th century's great media mergers—the more riveting for being a real love match—while the memory of her marriage to Miller simultaneously sexes up the intellectual playwright's image and complements the actress' own intellectual pursuits. (Her bookcase famously included first editions of Ralph Ellison and Jack Kerouac.)

But Marilyn the Legend eludes any new details or artifacts. By now the images we carry of her—skirt billowing over a subway grating, curves glinting in a poured-on, backless rhinestone dress as she sings "Happy Birthday, Mr. President" to JFK in a whipped-cream voice, silk-screened interpretive portrait by Andy Warhol—are as easily accessible in the mind as family pictures in a wallet. She is claimed as a member of the family by drag queens, feminists, and average joes alike. Everyone feels entitled to a piece of her. (Madonna at one time behaved as if she were channeling her.) And yet no one can capture her.

Of course, in the midst of such damp swoonery, a little dry air is welcome. "When I first met her at Strasberg," remembers classmate Shelley Winters, "she was very modest. She was much more relaxed and into having fun. We used to hang out at Schwab's—it was a famous drugstore where actors used to hang out. And we actually lived together for a little while." The thought of a relaxed, fun-loving girl at the malt shop with the other kids, all of them the bright future of American acting, is captivating enough. But that the unobtainable, doubt-tormented woman went on to signify everything sexy and vulnerable, glamorous and tragic in Hollywood, a star who mirrored as many different desires as there are desirers—ah, that's the "luminous quality" that eludes words, no matter how many literary garlands to Marilyn Monroe are piled like flowers to a dead princess. —LISA SCHWARZBAUM

MAKING WAVES (This page) bathing beauty Monroe has a splashy role in her final, uncompleted film, 1962's *Something's Got to Give*; (opposite page) the platinum screen siren hits the town in full glamour mode in 1959

PHOTOGRAPHS BY WILLIAM READ WOODFIELD

SIMPLY
THE BEST

JAWS (1975)
Who cares if his great
white feeding frenzy
ushered in the garish
summer blockbuster
era? It's still a white-
knuckled masterpiece.
*"You're gonna need a
bigger boat."*

▲ *CLOSE ENCOUN-
TERS OF THE THIRD
KIND* (1977)
This paranoid precursor
to *The X-Files* is where
we learned that the
truth was out there...

*RAIDERS OF THE
LOST ARK* (1981)
Reaching back to
adventure serials,
he gave us Indiana
Jones, the fedora-
sporting swashbuckler
every kid wants to
grow up to be.

SCHINDLER'S LIST
(1993)
With this powerful and
gut-wrenching Holocaust
drama, Spielberg came
of age as a mature,
complex storyteller. It
won him his first—and
long overdue—Best
Director Oscar.

*SAVING PRIVATE
RYAN* (1998)
More than 50 years
after the war ended,
Spielberg realistically
fired off the alpha and
omega of WWII films—
which earned him his
second directing Oscar.

steven
Spielberg

IT HAS ALL THE ELEMENTS OF THE QUINTES-
sential Steven Spielberg movie. Eye-pop-
ping special effects. A miraculous journey
through space and time. A lost childlike
creature searching for a way home.
✦ We're talking about *The Wizard of Oz*,
not *E.T.: The Extra-Terrestrial*—but then,
the two films do have a lot in common. In
fact, if you think about it, *E.T.* is really just
Oz inverted: A wayward munchkin crash-
lands on Earth, where three sweetly innocent locals (and their little dog, too) help
him find a way back to his no-place-like-
home planet. *E.T.*'s spaceship even zooms
over a rainbow at the end. ✦ Think about
it further, and something else becomes
clear: No director in the last 50 years has
captured the essence of *Oz*—its corn-fed
American wholesomeness, its wonder of
magic, its joy at the power of movies to
transport us to worlds beyond imagination—more than that bearded, bespecta-
cled brainiac who's brought dinosaurs and
aliens to life. In the Lollipopland of Holly-

4

wood, Spielberg really is the all-powerful wizard behind the curtain, a cinematic magician with plenty of heart (a big red blinking one in *E.T.*), lots of brains (he wrote *Close Encounters of the Third Kind* backward, from ending to beginning, and still wound up with one of the smartest sci-fi flicks ever made), and sometimes even courage.

In recent years, Spielberg has branched beyond spinning enchanting fairy tales, turning his camera toward the most solemn subject matter imaginable, the twin horrors of war and genocide. But even these shockingly powerful pictures—*Saving Private Ryan* and *Schindler's List*—have a touch of sorcery to them. They are, in fact, Spielberg's greatest miracles: Who else but the world's most commercial director could turn a three-hour black-and-white drama about the Holocaust into one of the most popular fact-based films in history (grossing $320 million worldwide)? Who but a master of fantasy could capture the reality of battle more brutally or viscerally, and with enough artistry to again dominate a year's box office?

"I knew when I saw the movie that Steven had dragged us into something that was *much* bigger than the sum of its parts," *Ryan* star Tom Hanks recalls of his bracing first view of the film. "I was emotionally crippled by it. I had to sit in my car afterwards. I couldn't even drive."

From the beginning of his career, it was obvious Spielberg possessed potential far beyond that of ordinary 24-year-old first-time directors. His debut, a 1971 TV movie called *Duel*—in which Dennis Weaver matched wits with a deadly diesel truck—was so well received it was eventually released in theaters here and abroad. His first genuine theatrical release, 1974's *Sugarland Express*—in which Goldie Hawn matched wits with pretty much the entire state of Texas—got the endorsement of even the notoriously hard-nosed Pauline Kael. ("This film is one of the most phenomenal debut films in the history of movies," she gushed.)

But it wasn't until 1975, with the opening of *Jaws*, that the world felt the full force of Spielberg's power. That little fish tale became the biggest hit of its time, the first film to gross more than $100 million domestically. By today's standards, that figure might have a quaint pinkie-to-the-mouth, Dr. Evil-esque ring to it, but back then it was enough to shake Hollywood in ways it's never gotten over. The entire Event Movie phenomenon of the last 20 years—with studios now spending $100 million a picture hoping to build the next largest-ever blockbuster—can all be traced back to Spielberg's notoriously malfunctioning mechanical shark.

Spielberg, of course, went on to shake Hollywood some more, with 1977's *Close Encounters* (grossing $337 million worldwide), 1981's *Raiders of the Lost Ark* ($386 million), and 1982's *E.T.* ($705 million). Altogether, his 18 films—including those two little-known art-house pieces, *Jurassic Park* and its sequel, *The Lost World*—

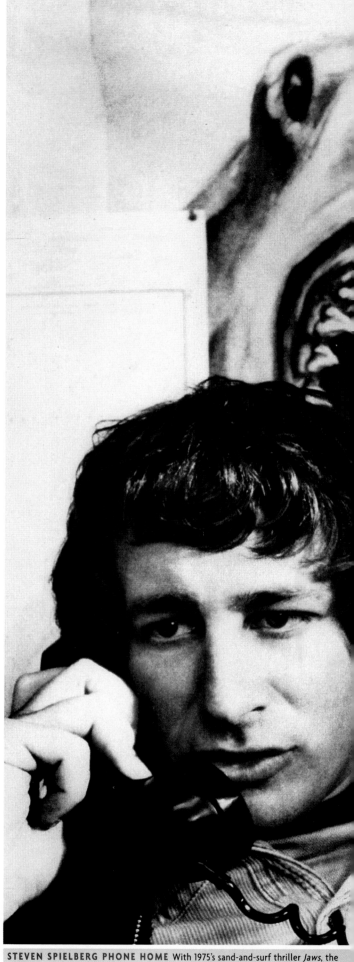

STEVEN SPIELBERG PHONE HOME With 1975's sand-and-surf thriller *Jaws*, the

8-year-old director single-handedly created the summer event movie phenomenon

have grossed more than $2.5 billion, making him one of the most financially successful filmmakers ever.

And yet even in Spielberg's most popcorny efforts there is usually something personal—some little sliver of himself—spooled onto the reels. In his early films, you can find shadows of his childhood phobias (he's publicly admitted to being terrified of the water; presumably he's not too keen on trucks, either). In other movies, there are hints of his broken home life growing up in Arizona and Northern California (behind the special effects of *Close Encounters* is a heartbreaking portrait of a family crumbling).

Critics have sometimes complained that his movies are too calculatedly commercial and gimmicky. But even his more mechanical efforts—the ones with the lawyer-chomping T. rex and snot-blowing brontosaurs—say something about Spielberg's imagination. "You can feel his brilliance palpably when you're working with him," Jeff Goldblum recalls of his experiences shooting both *Jurassic Park* and *The Lost World*. "He's supremely confident—even when he doesn't know what he's doing. He doesn't mind not knowing. He's willing to say, 'Okay, let's just make it up.' It's part of what makes him so great and so creative."

Other critics have complained that Spielberg is too manipulative, that he shamelessly toys with people's emotions. Maybe so. But isn't manipulating the audience—making us laugh or cry or scream with nothing more than flickering lights on a wall—what filmmaking is all about? What's different about Spielberg is that he's often more playful about it—and always more adroit. Any director can draw tears from a death scene; how many can leave an audience weeping over the fate of an animatronic alien with a face like an overgrown gallbladder? As Spielberg's onetime protégé Robert Zemeckis puts it, "It's like writing a review of a roller coaster and trashing it for being too scary."

In any case, Spielberg's detractors have been mostly silent lately. Whatever doubts they may have had about his gravity as a director were washed away by *Schindler's List* and *Saving Private Ryan*. With both films, Spielberg trained his technical brilliance on savagely serious, profoundly personal, and utterly uncommercial material. The result: While *Schindler* earned him his long-deserved first Academy Award, *Ryan* was celebrated as nothing less than a sacred new national monument (which, come to think of it, maybe it is).

What marvels this wizard will perform over the next decade or two—and doubtless there will be plenty; he is, after all, 53—no crystal ball can reveal. And that may be the ultimate trick up Spielberg's sleeve: He never fails to surprise in ways that are unmistakably his own. He's taken us places no other director has ever dreamed of—cinematic poppy fields of Technicolor magic, about as far from Kansas as anyone could possibly imagine—and yet somehow they've always felt sublimely, irresistibly familiar. In fact, they've felt a lot like home. —BENJAMIN SVETKEY

Madonna

ELVIS WANTED TO SOUND LIKE NO ONE ELSE. THE BEATLES WANTED to crack rock & roll open like a psychedelic walnut and make un-heard-of music from its meat and shards. But what, to narrow down Freud's famous question, does Madonna want? She has always want-ed—*wants*—to be famous; music is, for her, a means to an end, one method among many. Which is not to say that the music she's made isn't good, and sometimes great (both "Like a Virgin" and "Justify My Love" ought to fit any sensible person's definition of classic pop singles), but rather that music is just one aspect of her appeal. It is an appeal—controversial, to be sure, and perennially in danger of flam-ing out—which has lasted into three decades now. There is no doubt that Madonna, 41, is, among other things, the most significant female performer pop culture has produced in the last half of the 20th cen-tury—and arguably the most written about and most analyzed pop figure after those Beatles and that Elvis. Yet figuring out why this is so is half the fun. Vocalists from Billie Holiday to Aretha Franklin to Lauryn Hill have better pipes, and, depending on your taste, Marilyn Monroe, Susan Sarandon, or Britney Spears has exerted more sex appeal. But no one has ever combined voice, sex appeal, and an avid, always-questing artistic vision in the way Madonna Ciccone has. All this, plus she's made the kabbalah hip, Sandra Bernhard look like a groupie, and more good music videos than anyone, female *or* male.

Madonna came up through the usual showbiz ranks: took dance lessons at 13; fooled around in a rock band, the Breakfast Club, as guitarist and drummer (not, take note, lead vocalist—she's never been that hoariest of rock clichés, the "chick singer"); caught the tail end of disco in the early '80s. Disco, with its proud reliance upon mechanical artifice over artful authenticity, was the right medium for her. Early singles like "Everybody," "Lucky Star," and "Borderline" showcase a thin but urgent voice, and the videos that accompanied them display a neo-ragamuffin with ferocity brim-ming in her heavily mascara'd eyes.

"The thing that struck me right away about her was that she said she had no heroes," says Reggie Lucas, the producer-guitarist who wrote "Borderline" and produced her 1983 debut *Madonna*. "When I pressed her for influences, she said 'Michael Jackson,' and I remem-ber thinking, Okay, I understand now—you want to be a complete en-tertainer, not just a singer." Adds Lucas, who has worked with Miles Davis and produced hits for singers such as Stephanie Mills and Phyl-lis Hyman: "She was one of the first pop singers to deal with black music in a serious way. In fact, in the beginning it was most impor-tant to her to break a hit record in the black community, because she knew that would give her credibility throughout the *entire* indus-try—she's very shrewd that way."

Shrewd, but not, according to Lucas, another popular stereotype. "I've worked with divas, and Madonna was no diva, at least at that point," says Lucas, adding that her inherent faith in herself paid off for her collaborators. "Have you ever noticed how few performers, especially women—because they have to work harder for creative credit—rarely give props to their producers? Madonna always gave her producers public credit—it's part of her self-confidence.

"One thing always bugs me," Lucas continues. "People say she doesn't have 'a good voice.' I say, hey, it's what you do with what you've got, and when you listen to those early hits, she was willing to take chances with her voice and her material that people with trained, or more conventionally 'good,' voices would do."

Disco turned out queens a dime a dozen; none of them, not even Donna Summer, lasted much beyond their genre. Madonna did, be-cause she was always multitasking: churning out radio tunes and dance remixes with producers like Jellybean Benitez and Patrick Leonard, but also behaving like a little Donna Karan, designing her own mix 'n' match fashion sense that inspired millions of mimicking material girls to turn themselves into what the media were happy to label "Madonna wannabes." Having attracted both a chic dance-club following and a broad teenybopper fan base, Madonna just kept on expanding. Her first major movie, 1985's *Desperately Seeking Su-san*, played off her then-current wisecracking-urchin image, but the film's success made middle-aged moviegoers take notice as well—again, it's all about audience expansion, with plenty of craft and just enough art to stifle the more dismissive critics.

Which is to say, most of them. For unlike the Beatles or Elvis, Madonna has had to endure a degree of critical calumny that moves well beyond knee-jerk misogyny (*this little disco dolly—why, she can't even sing!*) into an interesting area. By process of multimedia elimination, rock critics were the writers that regularly evaluated Madonna's work, and she threatened their most vaunted critical

PHOTOGRAPHS (PREVIOUS PAGES) BY INEZ VAN LAMSWEERDE AND VINOODH MATADIN

LUCKY STAR (1) Madonna as a bambino in '78; (2) the Material Girl makes the over-accessorized look popular for a generation of wannabes; (3) in '90 she switches to extreme couture for the Blonde Ambition tour; (4) performing Down Under in '93; (5) returning to her roots as a brunette in '98

precept: "authenticity," the notion that the star *is* her or his persona (see freshman college class "Bruce Springsteen 101").

But Madonna positively reveled in her *in*authenticity. "The whole reason I got into show business wasn't because I thought I had a spectacular voice," she told an MTV interviewer. "It was because I thought I had something to say." She never made any bones about using disco as a stepping-stone, not as an aesthetic manifesto; her idea of a confessional song was "Papa Don't Preach," which may have been a loosely derived reference to her father's strict upbringing but also served as a taunt to critics both professional (don't tell me what or how to sing) and civilian (don't tell me what I shouldn't sing about in a song—in this case, abortion). Her brief marriage to another feisty, who-cares-what-the-critics-think type, actor Sean Penn (married in '85; divorced in '89), only seemed to bolster Madonna's resolve to do things her own way. Indeed, her 1990 tour was dubbed Blonde Ambition as a double nose-thumbing: She wasn't a "real" blond, and unlike those then-revered blokes in U2, she asserted that there was nothing wrong with proclaiming one's ambition, as opposed to making superstardom seem like an unintended side effect of baring one's soul.

The 1991 documentary made about the tour, *Truth or Dare*, was Madonna's way of being candid. She devised a movie that was supposedly behind-the-scenes frank stuff (temper tantrums! hand-holding prayers before performances! giggling sessions with gay boys!), but it was stuff that was controlled with steely assurance by Herself. The most revelatory comment in the movie is made by her then–boy toy, Warren Beatty, the eternal control freak who cowers from the intrusion of the lens, but not before saying, "She doesn't want to *live* off camera." Beatty was only helping this process along when he cast her opposite himself in 1990's *Dick Tracy*, an interesting hit that Madonna followed with a box office grand slam, 1992's jaunty baseball flick *A League of Their Own*.

In fact, bearing in mind Beatty's quote, we notice that she spent the early '90s living in front of cameras of all sorts. The still cameras that took the shocking shots that became the corrosive 1992 coffee-table book *Sex* were more kind to her than the movie-studio ones that recorded her in the film bomb *Body of Evidence* the next year. Combined with '92's uneven, jaded-sounding CD, *Erotica*, it began to look as if it might be a good time to sell your Madonna stocks short.

But, newly pregnant when she began shooting a dream project, the 1996 film of *Evita*, Madonna might as well have named her kid Tenacity instead of Lourdes. *Evita* was a middling profit maker but a small triumph of Madonna-brand brio, and after a year or so of motherhood and yoga, her *Ray of Light* managed a few unexpected feats: It was a return to dance music—now a creamy techno blend, courtesy of producer William Orbit. And it was a hit at a time when she was supposed to have been eclipsed by younger female acts like Alanis Morissette (signed to Madonna's adventuresome, profitable boutique label, Maverick), Courtney Love, and the Spice Girls.

Her secret? Unlike most entertainers who ascend to superstardom, Madonna never grows complacent; recognition of artistic legitimacy is important to her, but so is her ongoing role as pop-culture provocateur—oh, let's just say it plainly: irritant. The girl likes to get under our skin. Thus we have moments sprinkled through her career such as her performance at the first MTV Video Music Awards in 1984, a few minutes spent writhing around the stage in a white wedding gown yowling "Like a Virgin"; or her notoriously expletive-filled 1994 appearance on David Letterman's show (had it been a male star, he'd have been written off as a goofball on a bender, but this was Madonna, and so her bawdiness was supposed to Mean Something—but what?); or her recent evolution as a British-accented grande dame: Meryl Streep with a thang for Austin Powers.

Ah, so much Madonna, so little time. So many reasons to never count her out. —K T

TRUTH OR DARE (1991)
Fun documentary in which Madonna proves she's a witty harpy; added bonus: embarrasses then-paramour Warren Beatty on camera

RAY OF LIGHT (1998) ▶
CD reestablishes her as a dance-music force to be reckoned with.

frank Sinatra

WHEN FRANK SINATRA WAS READY TO SING, HE was ready, and to be in his way was...inadvisable. ✦ That's a lesson Brad Garrett learned from his first night opening for Sinatra in Vegas. In his stand-up days, which coincided with Sinatra's final touring years, Garrett, now renowned as the cop brother on *Everybody Loves Raymond*, learned right away to expect the unexpected. "Usually when you opened for somebody, they'd tell you to do 25 minutes, and it was very structured," says the basso-profundo-voiced comic. "With him, it would change every night." ✦ "The first week, his people said, 'Do 15 to 25.' I said, 'But how do I know?' They said, 'Oh, you'll know.' So I was out there, and about 15 minutes in, Frank just walks out and starts singing 'Luck Be a Lady,' right in the middle of my bit. Then he grabs my mike, puts his arm around my shoulder, and goes, 'Greg Barrett, everybody, Greg Barrett! Isn't he marvelous?' He whispers in my ear, 'Kid, I gotta get back to the Springs. You can do more tomorrow. GREG BARRETT!'" ✦ It wasn't the last time

Sinatra would mangle his opening act's name, but "of course I didn't have the balls to correct him," Garrett admits. "What are you gonna say, 'Frank, read the marquee!'?" ✦ Much less, "Frank, watch the clock"? Not when it was Sinatra's consuming impatience that worked to the aesthetic benefit of hundreds of millions of music fans. In the studio, he was a notoriously painstaking stickler for getting it right, plowing through as many takes as it took until the right arrangement or turn of phrase stuck. In concert, though, looseness and spontaneity were the rule, and all that mattered was being in the moment. The Chairman, like so many great artists—and not a few terrible ones—operated on his own clock. It was Sinatra standard time, and the rest of us just went ring-a-ding-ding on it. ✦ His boredom at the thought of singing even a signature number the same way twice was at the heart of his gift and goes a long way in explaining why, in bootleg shops around the world, you can find illicit concert recordings of Sinatra alongside the exhaustively cataloged live

work of Springsteen, Dylan, and the Dead, but not, say, a fine but predictable stylist like Tony Bennett. It's been theorized that no one alive actually knows the correct words to "The Lady Is a Tramp" just because Sinatra has riffed on them so many different ways. Even in the September of his years, when his vocal powers and memory for lyrics (and opening acts) were beginning to desert him, he was full of spit, vinegar, and surprises.

A lot of the surprises were extramusical, of course. The skinny kid from Hoboken, N.J., recorded some 1,200 songs over six decades before his death in 1998 at 82, and it's safe to say no one endured the glare of the spotlight longer than Sinatra. The Beatles may have broadened our notion of celebrity, but Sinatra virtually invented it, beginning around the time he made millions of WWII-era bobby-soxers scream out of their heads, setting the scene for Elvisteria. He lived hard, loved rough, swaggered, brawled, cozied up to mobsters and Presidents, and flipped the finger at the press who turned his every move into headlines. He made a spectacular comeback long before John Travolta. And in his fierce support of John F. Kennedy, he forged a glitzy Hollywood–Washington connection long before Warren Beatty.

The voice—The Voice—would've been legacy enough. Sinatra came of age as a heartthrob baritone with Tommy Dorsey in the early '40s, but it wasn't long into his first solo contract with Columbia that he began changing the face of popular singing, treating his voice like another instrument in the band, with all the swoops and sly dips that were usually the province of the trombone player

or trumpeter. In Sinatra's breakthrough records, pure expressiveness finally bested formality—and so went the century.

It's his emotion-laden '50s Capitol recordings that carry the most cachet today, many of them cut with Nelson Riddle. The peak of their collaboration, 1956's *Songs for Swingin' Lovers!*, has aptly been referred to by Sinatra scholar Will Friedwald as "the final statement on pre-rock pop. Something radically different just had to come next because nothing in the realm of Tin Pan Alley could top this bravura celebration of grown-up love." Even some of rock's seeming thematic advances had little on Sinatra: He was boldly making concept albums decades before *Journey to the Centre of the Earth* was a gleam in Rick Wakeman's eye. Who else would've had the nerve to put together a collection of pitiful laments under a title like *No One Cares*? Boohoo classics like *In the Wee Small Hours* and *Only the Lonely* spoke to the Everyman inside us all: If a winner like Frank could get this forlorn, and not off himself, there was hope for us lesser mortals to survive *our* Ava Gardners.

"That was his forte, the lonesome thing," says Bill Miller, who was Sinatra's pianist for four decades, collaborating on small-scale masterpieces like "One for My Baby." "It worked, didn't it? Don't forget, he wasn't a 'jazz singer.' He countered the lost-love songs with some of the so-called swingin' things, but he was a *balladeer*. That's what he did best."

He did some lesser tasks astonishingly well, too—like winning an Academy Award for acting. Not every picture was a *From Here*

to *Eternity* or *The Manchurian Candidate*, but even *The Tender Trap*-style froth could have wide-screen fun with his bachelor image and could maybe, incidentally, drop a swell new theme song into the lexicon.

The '70s and '80s weren't so kind, as notorious rock hater and recent Republican convert Sinatra came to represent the antithesis of the singer-songwriter movement and most "progressive" political showbiz thought. It didn't help that his once-impeccable taste in material waned during his Reprise years. The greatest pop singer of the century, a tireless crusader against racism before it was the thing to do, seemed a little more like a dinosaur every time "My Way" got a self-defensive spin, and further revelations made it abundantly clear that misogyny wasn't just a function of his *Ocean's Eleven* persona. Even some of the recent pro-Sinatra revisionism has reveled in Rat Pack campiness more than in celebrating his real gifts.

Given that the tenderness he managed on record wasn't his trademark outside the studio, few would dispute that—when the brickbats really started flying his way—he had a lot of it coming. Still, the Kitty Kelley bio and the *Rat Pack* telefilm failed to see the soulful forest for the pugilistic trees. "The HBO thing was ridiculous and so overly accentuated," complains writer Bill Zehme, who worked with the crooner during his declining years on a celebrated book about style, *The Way You Wear Your Hat*. "If Sinatra was that big of an a--hole, why would anybody want to be near him? He was actually a lot of fun to be around, and you didn't

get that from [Ray] Liotta's performance. If you go by that, you'd think everybody must have quivered in terror to be near him, which is unfortunate."

Indeed, from the 1960s onward, Sinatra fostered an enviable sense of showbiz community, submerging his former lonely-guy persona in a good-time pack mentality—and if it was mostly a "No Girls Allowed" pack, at least he displayed a generosity of spirit about sharing the spotlight. "Even in the last few years, it was the Rat Pack feel," says Garrett. "He would do a show, and [then] he would go out to a lounge, go see other performers, take us out to dinner.... It was a camaraderie that doesn't exist in Hollywood today."

One thing's certain: No one's about to assume the mantle. Occasionally someone like Latin-music sensation Marc Anthony will get the "new Sinatra" tag—and immediately slough it off, lest he appear to harbor delusions of grandeur. "Frank Sinatra's Frank Sinatra, man," says an admiring Anthony. "His phrasing's absolutely impeccable. I don't know what metronome he was on in his head, but it was a totally different metronome from the band"—speaking of Sinatra operating on his own clock—"and it would always sit where it needed to sit.... Guys like that only come around once in a hundred years."

Hey, the 21st century should be so lucky. Here's guessing that a hundred years from now, for millions of music lovers who care to remember but are drinking to forget, it'll still be Frank Sinatra getting under their skin. —CHRIS WILLMAN

7 Saturday

LIVE WIRES (1) Fernando (Crystal) and Ed
ley (Short); (2) nerds Murray and Radner
eyeful; (3) Mayor Giuliani visits Shannon,
Mary Katherine Gallagher, and Oteri; (4) Ros
Roseannadanna; (5) Rock and Farley are h
(6) Shannon and John Goodman skewer the L
sky scandal; (7) Carvey's Church Lady; (8) The
heads; (9) Meadows; (10) Gallagher is a *supe*
(11) frequent host Steve Martin; (12) Honeyro
Murphy and Piscopo; (13) Anal Retentive Chef
man; (14) guests Bruce Springsteen, Tom H
(15) producer Michaels with Cher and B
(16) Roseanne guests; (17) at the Olympia re
rant; (18) Aykroyd, Belushi; (19) Smalley's
enough; (20) coffee talk, anyone?

Night Live

IT WAS THE FALL OF '75, THE ATMOSPHERE WAS CHARGED, AND A little New York-based TV show, *Saturday Night Live*, made its debut. Then it was canceled one year later.

We speak of ABC's now-forgotten *Saturday Night Live With Howard Cosell*, a variety show hosted by the esteemed sports broadcaster. But also in 1975, just a couple weeks later, with practically no fanfare, another variety show snuck onto the tube. "I suggested we call ours *Saturday Night Live Without Howard Cosell*," says original cast member Chevy Chase. "But that didn't work."

The punchline, of course, is that more than 25 years later, this second show—*NBC's Saturday Night*, as it was called back then—has yet to say buh-bye. Instead, it's grown from TV rebel to institution, spawned at least 42 catchphrases ("Oh, nooo, Mr. Bill!" "Jane, you ignorant slut," "Never mind," and "You look mahvehlous," to name a few), gone through more than 70 cast members, made at least four comebacks, poked fun at five sitting Presidents, endured one papal-photo tearing, weathered three on-air *f---*s, and survived an appearance by Steve Forbes. In short, it's become the longest-running, most influential show in American comedy.

What's the secret to its bizarrely extended shelf life? Let's see: How about its ongoing commitment to embrace the zeitgeist— yeah, that's the ticket. Equally important, *SNL* creator and executive producer Lorne Michaels cleverly rejected the idea of a permanent host (NBC suggested that hip, young Candice Bergen anchor the show), which meant there wasn't anyone for fickle viewers to get tired of. Rather, *SNL* became a revolving door for comedians—some brilliant, some hacks, but always new. "It's not a show as much as it is a format," says former *SNL* writer Robert Smigel, the man behind those animated crime fighters The Ambiguously

Gay Duo. "All the headlines that said *Saturday Night Dead* missed the point. It's just an opportunity for every generation to express themselves in a 90-minute, Don Pardo-announced platform."

And my, how they've expressed themselves. Just look at a few of the stars who've passed through Studio 8H: Samurai/Killer Bee John Belushi; his partner-in-blues Dan Aykroyd; the queen of eccentric rants, Gilda Radner; Bill Murray, in all his smarmy splendor; that renegade Gumby/Mr. Robinson, Eddie Murphy; polysyllabic sarcasm master Dennis Miller; Adam Sandler, with his goofy, childish Operaman; basement-dwelling schwing-ers Mike Myers and Dana Carvey; news faker Norm Macdonald; Molly Shannon, with her kiss-starved Catholic schoolgirl; not to mention Chevy Chase, Jane Curtin, Billy Crystal, Martin Short, Joe Piscopo, Phil Hartman, David Spade, Chris Farley, Chris Rock…and, of course, Gary Kroeger and his hilarious appearances as Needleman the Dentist.

Okay, so not everything was a knee-slapper. But what other TV show has had such remarkable range, even within the span of a single episode? As current cast member Tim Meadows says, "Lorne Michaels sprinkles a little political humor, a little Generation X comedy, a little conceptual comedy, a little character comedy. He mixes it up and allows performers to shine."

And for the many who did shine, the show itself became a launching pad to mainstream stardom. "People from radio like Hope and Crosby brought this other kind of energy [to the movies]," says Michaels, who produced many of the films starring *SNL* cast members. "I thought, that would be fun to do with TV people." Fun and insanely profitable. Chase was the first to leave the series, finding commercial success in features like *Caddyshack*. After him came Belushi and Aykroyd in *The Blues Brothers*, then

SIMPLY THE BEST

LAND SHARK ▶
(NOV. 8, 1975)
An ongoing parody of *Jaws*. Chevy is the intruding predator ("Candygram"); Laraine and Jane are his victims.

KING TUT SONG ▶
(APRIL 22, 1978)
Protesting the "commercialization" of the Tutankhamen exhibit, Steve Martin performs his ode to the boy king.

TO ALL A GOOD *NIGHT* (1) Sweeney is the androgynous Pat with guest Harvey Keitel; (2) fops join Macdonald's "Weekend Update"; (3) two wild and crazy guys Martin and Aykroyd; (4) early *SNL* players, from left, Murray, Curtin, Radner, Morris, and Newman; (5) Spartan Cheerleaders Ferrell and Oteri; (6) Wayne (Myers) and Garth (Carvey) party on, dude; (7) Killer Bees Belushi, Chase, and Radner help create a buzz for the show in the early days.

Murphy in *48 HRS.*, right on up to last summer's blockbusters from Myers (*Austin Powers: The Spy Who Shagged Me*) and Sandler (*Big Daddy*). All told, the show's alums have raked in more than $3 billion at the box office, making *SNL* the most profitable finishing school in the business.

Of course, the original Not Ready for Prime Time Players would have never embraced such an establishment goal. They considered themselves comedy radicals—young, dangerous, and fighting against the middle-of-the-road, cornpone shtick of Johnny Carson et al. (In fact, Carson did despise them, attacking the show for relying on drug jokes and cruelty, and noting that the cast couldn't "ad-lib a fart at a bean-eating contest.") And when it started, *SNL* truly was like nothing else on TV. The very first sketch—which had writer Michael O'Donoghue teaching John Belushi English phrases such as "I would like to feed your fingertips to the wolverines"—made that instantly clear. One of those watching was Steve Martin, then touring the country as a wild and crazy stand-up. As he recounts in Doug Hill and Jeff Weingrad's book, *Saturday Night*, Martin remembers saying to himself, "F---. They did it. They did the show everyone should have been doing."

This wasn't Carol Burnett doing Scarlett O'Hara with a curtain rod. This was absurd, slightly violent, death-tinged stuff. This was Aykroyd as a badly cut Julia Child geysering blood all over the studio. This was Garrett Morris appropriating racial and cultural stereotypes as washed-up Dominican ballplayer Chico Escuela ("Bessbol been berry berry goo to me"). This was Chase making tasteless "Weekend Update" jokes about everything from expired dictators to oral sex. "We had a little trick," says Chase. "During dress rehearsal, when the censor was in the studio, [O'Donoghue]

would stand in front of him and ask him a question just as the joke was coming, and the censor would never hear the joke."

It was that boundary-pushing mind-set, combined with the intensive comedy-cramming sessions (Martin Short says "it's like final exams every week," and former writer Anne Beatts has referred to it as "a combination of summer camp and concentration camp"), that led Chris Rock to call *SNL* "the Harvard of comedy."

And as many a legitimacy-hungry host and street-cred-craving rock act can tell you, *SNL* also has a knack for conferring an advanced degree of coolness. Consider this: What other show could have enticed the likes of Nancy Kerrigan, Sinéad O'Connor, and Monica Lewinsky in front of a rowdy audience full of hard-bitten New Yorkers?

But an aura of hipness never prevented the show from having a good laugh at itself. Consider the now-famous Killer Bees. Though the insects bombed badly in *SNL*'s first episode, they bravely returned in a show hosted by *All in the Family*'s Rob Reiner. "I was told when I came on the show that I would not have to work with the bees," said Reiner, breaking character mid-sketch. An antennae-adorned Belushi snapped back: "You've got Norman Lear and a first-rate writing staff. But this is all they came up with for us."

The funny thing is—with or without the bees—*SNL*, more than any other TV series of our generation, has generated the most buzz around the watercooler. That's because, good or bad, the show has been a constant in our weekend schedules for a quarter of a century—a sometimes shocking, occasionally provocative, unavoidably addictive high-wire act brought weekly into our living rooms.

Imagine what it could have done with Cosell. —A.J. JACOBS

SYNCHRONIZED ▶ SWIMMING (OCT. 6, 1984)
A mockumentary where Harry Shearer and Martin Short try to turn men's synchronized swimming into an Olympic sport.

STAR TREK CONVENTION (DEC. 20, 1986)
The *Enterprise*'s Captain Kirk, a.k.a. William Shatner, snaps and berates a crowd of his geeky fans: "Get a life, will you, people! I mean, for crying out loud, it was just a TV show.... So move out of your parents' basements, get your own apartments, and grow the hell up."

CHIPPENDALES DANCERS (OCT. 27, 1990)
A lean Patrick Swayze faces off against a bulky Chris Farley in an exotic-male-dancer audition.

THINK OF HIM THEN, IN 1969, HYPERKINETICALLY bopping on *The Ed Sullivan Show*: the tiny boy from Gary, Ind., with a voice as huge as his Afro; a kid so gifted, some assumed he was a midget pretending to be a boy (in reality, he was an 11-year-old impersonating an 8-year-old). Think of him in 1983, moonwalking across a stage, so otherworldly and fluid he took a nation's breath away. Or think of him as the bastard child of Sammy Davis Jr. and Judy Garland, someone whose performances approach alchemy, whose artistry exceeds mere talent. ✦ That the name Michael Jackson doesn't immediately conjure such images—that he more often inspires thoughts these days of a freakish sideshow act—is entertainment's great tragedy. For all the glory of his spectacular showbiz ascent, from wonder child to Epic *Thriller*, it pales in comparison to his Icarus-like fall. Pet monkeys, supposed hyperbaric chambers, seemingly endless plastic surgery, skin lightening, surgical masks, ugly allegations of pedophilia, two failed marriages (the first to the daughter of pop's other King, the second to dermatology nurse Debbie Rowe, mother of his two children)—the stunning

8

michael

jackson

PHOTOGRAPH BY SAM EMERSON

list of eccentricities could only be topped in the tabloids by a former football star's alleged murder of his ex-wife.

Because of all this, and because Jackson has remained cloistered within the walls of his 2,700-acre Neverland ranch in Santa Ynez, Calif., for more than a decade—releasing just three albums to middling (for him) sales—it's tempting to use the past tense when talking about him. But if we convince you of one thing in this issue, it's that Michael Jackson should be celebrated for what he *meant* to share with us, rather than the media sideshow (though entertaining to some) he's become infamous for. "I don't look at it as he's not the hottest thing anymore—I look at what he's done as a groundbreaking artist who opened a lot of doors for black acts," says rapper Missy "Misdemeanor" Elliott, one of many hip-hop artists who cite him as an influence. "Michael Jackson is still amazing to me."

FROM THE MOMENT WE FIRST SAW HIM FRONTING THE JACKSON 5, belting out "I Want You Back" as if heartbreak and pain were nothing new to him, it was obvious this kid was more than a natural—he was preternatural. Motown president Berry Gordy Jr.—who released 7 of the group's top 10 singles—saw it instantly, and concluded that Michael was "a born star." God knows he had plenty of soul, more than any of his brothers, who weren't exactly soul slackers. But Michael had something else, something unquantifiable.

The extent of his gift became clearer in 1979, when Jackson made his first solo album, teaming up at Epic with producer Quincy Jones. If the result—the masterful, 7-million-selling *Off the Wall*—was a revelation (aging child star morphs into slick, sophisticated vocalist and songwriter, producing what *Rolling Stone* called "discofied post-Motown glamour at its classiest"), a subsequent tour was the *real* eye-opener. A self-conscious 21-year-old whose high-pitched whisper of a speaking voice hinted at affectations to come, Jackson was an enirely different animal on stage. His highly stylized phrasing and dancing were fiercely sexual and macho. The girls were starting to scream.

Off the Wall and its top 10 hits (including "Don't Stop 'Til You Get Enough," and "She's Out of My Life") confirmed Jackson as pop's prince. Then, in 1982 came his coronation. *Thriller*'s staggering success cannot be underestimated: It remains one of the best-selling albums of all time (more than 46 million copies worldwide), and Jackson won 8 of a possible 10 Grammy awards in '83. But the album's real significance lies in its wholesale obliteration of preconceived notions of "black" and "white" music. Its hits—"Billie Jean," "Human Nature," "Beat It"—became ubiquitous, embraced by soul lovers, casual pop fans, the burgeoning hip-hop nation, and rock enthusiasts. (The crossover appeal was something Jackson savvily orchestrated, recruiting frat-boy rocker Eddie Van Halen to contribute a searing lead guitar on "Beat It.") Even MTV had to pay attention: "Beat It" was the first video by a black artist to spin into heavy rotation, making Jack-

son a kind of Jackie Robinson of pop. And the 14-minute video of "Thriller," with MGM-worthy choreography, pushed the genre to astonishingly ambitious heights (it won three moonmen at MTV's first Video Music Awards).

In one fell swoop, Jackson had raised the bar for entertainers everywhere, and nascent megastars from Madonna to Prince were studying the young auteur. Clearly, he was the one to beat—but who, pray tell, was up to the task? He was a triple threat: gifted songwriter, vocalist, and dancer. When Jackson unveiled the moonwalk on Motown's 25th anniversary television special in '83, it rivaled man's first walk on the moon for stunning pop culture imagery. Talk about giant steps.

And how apt, really. For Jackson's talent and appeal—and he was the biggest star on the planet at this point—was indeed otherworldly. Crotch-grabbing aside, his androgynous man-child persona seemed to have dropped, *E.T.*-like, from the heavens. A supernatural pied piper for a new age, what could we do but follow?

BY 1988, HE'D FALLEN TO EARTH. BUBBLES WAS OUT, AND THE rumor mill was churning: The King of Pop was soon eclipsed by Wacko Jacko, a bizarro alter ego whose normalcy seemed to fade with his skin color. Many trees have been sacrificed to the question, What went wrong? Jackson had a crappy childhood of unremitting showbiz; his dad, Joe, would beat him up; he's got a sister named La Toya. Those are three good explanations. Really, though, who cares? Jackson's career can be seen as a morality tale, a Greek tragedy writ in tabloid headlines—the artist triumphant felled by ego unchecked. But we the audience are also complicit in the fall: Jackson is as pure a symbol as any of America's devastating plunge into the base pursuit of gossip and scandal. The naive fantasy is that if he can rise above it, couldn't we?

Word is Jackson's trying to do just that. His current handlers are busy fashioning a shiny new image for the star, one intended to put to rest his rep as a reclusive oddball. And he's working on his next album—with production chores handled by several hip young guns, including producer Rodney Jerkins. "Everybody talks about Madonna's ability to reinvent herself," says former *American Bandstand* host Dick Clark, a longtime friend and, like Elizabeth Taylor, outspoken supporter of Jackson. "Michael has that same ability, probably more so, because he's so extraordinarily talented. And when it comes to entertainment, that's been his whole life. I have no doubt he'll figure out the way to relaunch his career. For a man that didn't have much of a formal education, he's got a brilliant mind. He's a smart dude."

The falsetto-voiced Peter Pan is no pushover, that's for sure. Jackson's proven to be as shrewd a businessman as his erstwhile boss Berry Gordy. In 1984, the singer purchased Beatles catalog owners ATV Music Publishing Company for $47.5 million, angering his supposed buddy Paul McCartney. "I think it's dodgy to do things like that," griped McCartney at the time, "to be someone's

SUPER STAR A tiny boy with a voice as big as his Afro—a young Michael Jackson with a few of his favorite things in his bedroom in his onetime Encino, Calif., home.

friend and then to buy the rug they're standing on." Still, the deal paid Jackson 50 cents on the dollar every time a Beatles tune from the catalog was played (he merged his catalogs with Sony Music Publishing in '95). And he can be as ruthless as his take-no-bull dad. Just ask his brothers. For the past few years, they've been making noises about a J5 reunion. A great idea—if Michael is involved. "The truth is, in order to do it, they've got to have Michael," says Clark matter-of-factly, "and Michael has other priorities."

As the world awaits the next chapter of The Michael Jackson Sto-ry, the artist is ensconced in demanding (and highly hush-hush) ses-sions with Jerkins. "The stuff is incredible," promises the producer. "My goal [for the album] is to marry what I do to the older things he used to do, which was so melody rich. So just getting great melodies over my type of grooves with his voice, I think that would destroy everything out there. I don't think nothing can touch it...With Michael, we make sure it's perfect. He can't accept flaws." It's a tes-tament to Jackson's continued hold on us that, even at this late date, we're looking forward to being thrilled once more. —TOM SINCLAIR

lucille
Ball

OVER THE YEARS, HER WRITERS DEVELOPED A CODE. THEY'D invoke the shorthand name for some surefire bit of business in the stage directions, and Lucille Ball could run with it like a red-helmeted quarterback, unerring in her sense of how to parlay the call into a comedic touchdown. There was "the drats," a fists-clenched, double-forearm-drop gesture that Lucille's alter ego, Lucy—the starstruck showbiz-wannabe housewife forever wheedling her way onto stages and into celebrities' lives—would make after another crazy scheme backfired. Just as reliable was "the spider," that curl-the-upper-lip, swivel-the-head *"Eye-eeooooough!"* exclamation that said *Oh no* in a thousand ways. (It was so labeled because Ball first invented it playing a frightened Little Miss Muffett in late-'40s radio ads for Jell-O.) ✦ The thing that elevated these bits (and so many more never designated with any formal genus) beyond mechanical shtick and into perpetual-rerun touch-stones was the way Ball mixed them up and folded them into her Lucy characters with such seeming nonchalance, first as Mrs. Ricardo in her most enduring work, *I Love Lucy* (1951–57), then in *The Lucy–Desi Comedy Hour* (1957–60), *The Lucy Show* (1962–68), and *Here's Lucy* (1968–74). It was a magnificent illusion. People who worked with her knew that behind the impro-visatory aura, Ball was a compulsive rehearser who nursed every inch of her choreography till she knew it cold. She herself

9

rarely knew what was funny when handed a situation, but could she *play* that situation. The infamous putty-nose-on-fire gag? Totally planned (except the final touch of dipping her schnozz in a cup of coffee; that she added on set in a rare moment of improv). She once spent three hours practicing how to blow up and pop a paper bag for one momentary aside in an *I Love Lucy* segment.

The result, wrote *Lucy* producer-cowriter Jess Oppenheimer in his memoirs, was that "there was no feeling that the audience was watching her act. She simply *was* Lucy Ricardo. And if you looked carefully, you would marvel that every fiber in the woman's body was contributing to the illusion. Did Ricky catch her in a lie? She wouldn't be just a voice denying it. Her stance would be a liar's stance.... There would be a telltale picking at a cuticle, or a finger brushed against her upper lip.... Her hands, her feet, her knees— every cell—would be doing the right thing."

Though Ball made it look ineluctable, she stumbled into her slapstick métier only after spending the first half of her career fumbling around. Between the early '30s and the late '40s, she appeared in more than 60 movies, ranging from musicals (like *DuBarry Was a Lady*, the Technicolor flick that introduced her trademark, chemically induced electric-orange hair color) to melodramas (like *Stage Door*, opposite Katharine Hepburn and Ginger Rogers) to comedies (she bonded with Bob Hope on *Sorrowful Jones*). She plugged away but never became a top-tier, name-brand star.

By 1950, Ball had finally managed to peck out the one bona fide hit of her career—as a disembodied voice. She'd clicked big time in a radio show called *My Favorite Husband*, where she was the wacky wife of a staid banker (think *Dharma & Greg*). But radio was rapidly becoming a passé ghetto thanks to TV, which loomed at the start of the '50s the way the Internet does today. CBS wanted to translate Ball's radio show to TV, with Ball starring—and with her radio costar Richard Denning coming along for the ride.

That's when Ball (at 39!) gathered her strength and gambled everything. If CBS wanted a TV show, fine: She was going to use it to salvage not just her career but her life. Her 10-year marriage to Desi Arnaz, a Cuban bandleader five years her junior, was perpetually in danger of pulling apart due to their conflicting schedules. If she could just turn the TV gig into a chance for her and Desi to work together, she figured it might give them a sort of family life. So she dragged a nervous Desi into the nascent *I Love Lucy* as her costar, where he'd play a thinly fictionalized version of himself named Ricky Ricardo. Sponsors and network execs raised heated objections to the Arnaz casting. Who'd believe his character? they harrumphed. Lucille's ballsy response: You want me, you take my husband. Otherwise, no show.

It was the most unique form of couples therapy in the history of entertainment. And though it ultimately didn't work off camera— Lucille and Desi split for good in 1960, one day after filming their

last material as Lucy and Ricky—it worked miraculously well as fiction. By the end of its first, 35-episode season, *I Love Lucy* had regularly topped the weekly ratings. It was the season champion for the next three years and never left the top five in its entire run.

In the industry, *Lucy* changed everything: Not only did 30-minute sitcoms push aside variety hours as the dominant TV format, but the show's groundbreaking technique of shooting each episode on motion picture film with three cameras, then broadcasting the edited result (instead of beaming it out live with only a fuzzy kinescope as a record), was quickly adopted. That latter innovation was a happy accident born of Ball's refusal to do *Lucy* out of New York, then TV's capital. Arnaz proposed doing *Lucy* in an L.A. studio, but the network moguls felt Ball worked better with an audience. Okay, Arnaz impulsively countered, we'll shoot it in a studio on film with an audience. And since it's our demand, we'll pay the extra $5,000–6,000 per episode to do it that way— provided our fledgling company, Desilu, retains complete ownership of the films.

Thus the three-camera photography system, the "studio audience" for sitcoms, and the syndication market were all established in one serendipitous swoop. And as the broadcast infrastructure reeled, so did the public. *I Love Lucy* captivated post–World War II nest builders who were doing everything the Ricardos were doing: riding the power struggles of married life, trading up their apartments, moving to the suburbs. "There was no theatricality to it," says James L. Brooks, who spent the '70s replacing the Lucy family-comedy template with sitcoms built around workplaces. "You believed it was real. I mean, they had a baby on there and everything."

Behind the scenes, Ball was anything but just folks. She took over Desilu Productions after Desi, who was early on a business natural but became increasingly hobbled by alcoholism, bowed out in '62. And through the years, she grew impossibly bossy toward employees and costars alike (Joan Crawford, after guesting on an episode, said, "My God, and they say *I'm* a bitch"). Some of that ferociousness percolated beneath Ball's ditzy TV persona, but there it was actually endearing. *Lucy* plotlines centered an extraordinary amount of the time on fights. It was *Jerry Springer* and *The People's Court* with a happy ending, as the Ricardos constantly bickered over money and property, both with each other and with their neighbors Ethel (played to simmering perfection by Vivian Vance) and Fred Mertz (William Frawley, a crusty alcoholic whose hands were so shaky he had to keep them in his pants pockets—hence Fred's default stance).

It also didn't hurt that Ball, despite the public not being able to see her striking blue eyes and scarlet locks on their black-and-white sets, was about the hottest looker on the tube in her early days. Ball managed to make silly, physical comedy seem sexy— something no male clown had done before, certainly not Charlie Chaplin or Buster Keaton. (Many episodes ended with Lucy and

HAVING A BALL (1) Lucy has got some splainin' to do to hubby Ricky on the premiere of *I Love Lucy*. (2) A candy factory spells trouble for Lucy and Ethel (and bit player Elvia Allman) in the now-classic episode "Job Switching." (3) The consummate comedian gets a taste of her own medicine in the show's hilarious Vitameatavegamin skit.

Ricky en route to the bedroom, and even though the mattresses were separate, you just knew they ended up in one sack a lot.) "It's amazing, there was never any reference, or any other character who met her on that show, who ever thought she was attractive," marvels Brooks. "Nobody ever mentioned it. She was just regular. But of course she was so good-looking."

That was one of *Lucy*'s wonderfully subversive appeals. Lucy was ostensibly the untalented one, perennially kept out of showbiz by her successful bandleader husband. But every minute of the show proved otherwise. Arnaz could sing and act only passably (though he was a better arbiter off screen than Ball of what was funny), while Ball was a mesmerizing performer. "There's a delicious, secret pleasure in watching her challenge and completely upstage Ricky over and over," says feminist author Susan Faludi. "The spotlight was really on her. It was gratifying to so many women of that time who had to play the artificial role of second fiddle, the helpmate to their supposedly more competent, qualified husbands. It was a huge inside joke."

And a less-than-perfect fit for advertisers, who weren't exactly delighted that Ball was such a self-sufficient woman. (So much so that Saudi Arabia banned the show—'nuff said.) While Ball's clown act let her get away with murder on this front, after Lucy, most female TV characters were desexualized until Mary Tyler Moore and (more realistically still) Roseanne. The majority were insipid homemakers (Donna Reed, Jane Wyatt—even *That Girl*'s Marlo Thomas was a housewife in career-girl clothing), and until Carol Burnett, few were genuinely funny.

So Ball got the last laugh in many ways. On the outside, she was always deprecating herself with her "spider" wince. On the inside, we got the feeling that she never so much as blinked. As often as she wound up apologizing and kowtowing to Ricky Ricardo, it's not the Lucy who crumbled in the last 30 seconds we remember. We really loved the petulant, determined, scheming redhead who just couldn't do deferential. —STEVE DALY

the Simpsons

WAY BACK IN THE DAY—SAY, 36 YEARS AGO—LITTLE Matthew Groening would tool around with the neighborhood children in Oregon, building forts, reading comic books, and staging puppet plays. But while all the other boys and girls were giggling away these golden hours, our guy was filled with thoughts of doom. "The other kids—they were just playing," remembers Groening, 46. "They were going to move on to more mature subjects. Not me. I knew [playing] was all I was ever going to do, and I wasn't going to make a living out of it. My friends could draw better than me. My cartoons were ripped up by the teachers. I was told I was wasting my time. I figured I would be loading tires on a warehouse dock and drawing cartoons on the wall during breaks for the rest of my life."

✦ Oh, how eerily prophetic he was. (Well, except for that loading-tires-on-a-warehouse-dock part.) After doodling his way to alternative newspaper fame in the '80s with the beaten-down-bunnies strip *Life in Hell*, he unveiled a stroke of TV genius (cue white clouds, blue sky, ethereal choir):

The Simpsons. A spin-off of the variety series *The Tracey Ullman Show*, Fox's animated sitcom was a kidney punch of fresh air, juxtaposing happy-harmless animation with lickety-spitfire humor, and nary a canned laugh to massage the jokes. ✦ It was 1989, just two weeks before the turn of the decade, and change was in the air. Although *The Simpsons*' comedic and animation stylings were admittedly primitive ("We didn't know what we were doing," says Groening of year one), the show's impact on TV viewers was instantaneous: By season's end, Homer's Heroes had stormed up the Nielsens to No. 10, and the sunny-side-up *Cosby Show* was looking awfully tired. In the year 2000, some things have changed (Groening's baby is now a worldwide phenomenon, a billion-dollar empire—we're talking car mats, screensavers, *asthma inhaler sleeves*), but others are blissfully the same: A discriminating comedy that appeals indiscriminately, *The Simpsons* remains a popular *and* critical favorite. High-minded reviewers dig the brainy pop parodies; parents guffaw over the domestic strife;

their kids eat up the rebel humor and catchphrases ("Eat my shorts!"). Indeed, if any of TV's nuclear units can be dubbed our First Family, it's this maladjusted crew: boneheaded nuclear plant safety inspector Homer; his blue-haired moral compass, Marge; miscreant fourth-grader Bart; precocious second-grader Lisa; and pacifier-slurping Maggie. As they bumble their way through poignantly tweaked sitcom archetypes (in danger of failing history, Bart makes Homer proud by buckling down and earning a D minus), *The Simpsons* have defied and defined family-com convention.

One need only flip the TV dial to feel the torque of the show's wake—and we're not just talking about the current animation craze. The Simpsons created the prototype for '90s TV: the arch self-awareness of its target market; self-indulgent references to both pop and high culture; dead-on, dangerous farce; and the selling of dysfunction as mainstream. Shows as seemingly disparate as *South Park* and *Frasier* owe a debt to Homer and his brood. And where would today's teen movement be had *The Simpsons* not shown that youth-oriented didn't necessarily mean *D'oh!*?

None of this entirely explains, of course, why *The Simpsons*—the current longest-runnning prime-time comedy—has aged so well. Part of the answer lies in the show's unrivaled freedom, which Groening fought hard for from the beginning. Unlike so many of his sitcom-creating peers, he managed to keep his vision pure, resisting audience testing, research, and network fiddling. "Matt's a genuine iconoclast," says longtime *Simpsons* producer George Meyer. "He doesn't like any bridles, even socially prescribed ones. He's just an ornery guy who wants to go his own way."

And that's been a lifelong trend. At age 4—when the little rascal was already perusing *Playboy*, *Esquire*, and *The New Yorker*—Groening became obsessed with a Ronald Searle school-set comic featuring "torture and mayhem and arrows being shot and teachers' heads on pikes." At 7, while snooping in his parents' library, he stumbled upon an analytical text detailing the stages of child development. ("I read about ages 8, 9, and 10, and said, 'I'm not doing any of that stuff.'") At 17, hepped up on Frank Zappa records and Robert Crumb comics, he was elected student body president of Lincoln High School in Portland, Ore., after founding "Teens for Decency," which advocated either abolishing grades or letting students grade teachers.

When Groening grew up, not much changed. In creating *The Simpsons*, he subverted another tradition: the classic, wholesome family TV of his youth. "*Dennis the Menace* had this animated opening in which he came out of a hurricane," he notes, "and I was so thrilled there was going to be a kid on TV who was actually a menace, but then he turned out to be this sweet mild-mannered kid, and I was like, 'Hmmm….' I loved Eddie Haskell. I always thought he should be the star of *Leave It to Beaver*, you know? My whole grown-up career is about revisiting the entertainment of my childhood, but trying to do it like I wished it had been."

Fortuitously, he rounded up some crafty accomplices along the way. Codeveloped by *The Tracey Ullman Show*'s Sam Simon and

James L. Brooks of *Mary Tyler Moore Show* fame, The Simpsons assembled a staff of *Harvard Lampoon*-trained writers with enough collective brain wattage to short out a NASA lab. ("Lunchtime discussions can get a little boring," notes *Simpsons* exec producer Mike Scully. "Occasionally, I'd rather talk about hockey instead of mathematical arguments, you know?") These MAD scientists of comedy, whose ranks once included *Late Night* host Conan O'Brien and *King of the Hill* cocreator Greg Daniels, would forever smarten up the idiot box by thinking outside of it. Brooks recalls an early Groening epiphany: "One day Matt said, 'Nobody watches TV on TV. I think we have to be different about that.' I thought that was brilliant."

Consider life in Springfield, where fathers dismiss church as "boring," teachers are more interested in happy hour than paper grading, and Homer's perplexed reaction after being told he'll have to wait five days to buy a gun is "But I'm mad nowwwwwwww!" "A lot of sitcoms are earthbound and complacent," says Meyer. "They don't really want to shake up reality, they just want to gently spin it and then lovingly return it to its pedestal. We have a more nasty approach to life. We're social demolition men—we want

IN 'TOON Homer (1) hangs with U2 at Moe's, (2) gets to the point with Mel Gibson, and (3) rocks with the Ramones; (4) Lisa vegges out with Paul and Linda McCartney; (5) Sideshow Bob terrorizes Bart; (6) Marge and a pal channel *Thelma & Louise*; (7) Krusty the Clown puts on his act; (8) Homer spends quality time with his dad, Abe "Grampa" Simpson

to destroy institutions that aren't working anymore and toss them onto the junk heap. We're trying to teach people that it can be fun to use your intellect and question things."

Yet the wonderful irony of *The Simpsons* is that like the Trojan horse, it hides its greatest weapon: Within the cynical self-consciousness and clinical deconstruction is a mother lode of heart. "Matt never lost sight of the essential thing that made *The Simpsons* really good, which was, yeah, people love the really weird lines and everything, but what hooks you in is that you really believe that these people exist," says O'Brien. "If the show becomes too Ivy League smartass and too self-indulgent, then it all goes south. The reason the show is greater than the sum of its parts is because Matt knows this is a family that has real emotional connections to each other. And although that may not be the element that everybody recites, subliminally that's what keeps you coming back for the wiseass comments. What he supplied was something that you couldn't have gotten from *The Harvard Lampoon*, because they don't teach emotion in school."

That may be why people continue to send Groening photos of children in remote Amazon villages wearing "I'm Bart Simpson—Who the Hell Are You?" T-shirts. Or why *The Simpsons* is arguably the most successful TV show ever syndicated, with some seriously rabid fans taping it every night and rewinding repeatedly in hopes of catching a nanosecond gag. Or why it always trumps the snarky animated progeny that continue to spring up. "The problem with a lot of hip comedies is that, unconsciously or unintentionally, the message is 'Life is horrible and nothing matters,'" says Groening. "That may be true, but it's not as much fun as 'Life is wild and let's have a party.' Ultimately, the contradiction and ambivalence and joy and corruption and goofiness of America are worth celebrating and laughing at simultaneously."

Fair enough, but here's our reason for celebrating *The Simpsons*' success: It's a victory for every misunderstood underdog out there. "The teachers may have been right about my attitude problem, but for some reason, I still feel vindicated," chuckles Groening. "And I feel really lucky. I always wonder: Are people who have incredibly fortuitous careers aware of that? Or do they wake up going 'Oh no, another day?' Because I wake up every morning, going 'Yeah!!!! I'm not working in that tire warehouse!!!!'" —DAN SNIERSON

ROBERT ZIMMERMAN WAS BORN IN DULUTH, MINN., on May 24, 1941. He began performing folk songs under a name borrowed from Dylan Thomas, the poet, in '59. But—according to an anecdote near the heart of rock & roll history—Bob Dylan emerged full-grown at the Newport Folk Festival on July 25, 1965. There, having traded in his folkie work shirt for a hip leather jacket, he roared "Let's go!" and ripped electrically into "Maggie's Farm," bold-ly confirming the transformation of popular music.

As myth, the appeal of the Dylan-goes-electric sto-ry is its neat encapsulation of Dylan's particular na-ture: He is always, to borrow a line from "It's Alright, Ma (I'm Only Bleeding)," busy being born. "He was formulating himself as he went along," says D.A. Pen-nebaker, whose film *Don't Look Back* documents the months before Newport. "He didn't know where it was going to lead him." Early in his career, it led him to new frontiers of sound; since, it has led him to pur-sue his enigmatic genius around that strange terrain.

A self-titled 1962 album introduced the singular voice—by turns a nasal breeze, a caustic scoff, an earthy croon, a buoyant yawp. Placing evocative force before ordinary prettiness, Dylan redefined the singer's role. Then, on his next two albums (*The Freewheelin' Bob Dylan* and *The Times They Are A-Changin'*), remade as the most mystical of polit-ical songwriters, he reeled off such instantly classic protest songs as "Masters of War" and "The Lone-some Death of Hattie Carroll," hits that made him the proverbial spokesman for his generation. And with 1964's *Another Side of Bob Dylan*, he meta-morphosed into a spokesman for himself, ditching agitprop for poetry. As singer-songwriter Lucinda Williams says, "He brought together the tradition-al musical idiom of people like Woody Guthrie and the literary world of people like Allen Ginsberg."

Dylan is a trickster troubadour, a backyard absurd-ist whose lyrics are as expressive of feeling as they are evasive of understanding. (Even after a zillion spins, "Rainy Day Women #12 & 35" remains beau-tifully inscrutable.) Yet the contours of his lines—of lyrics that are intimately surreal, minutely narra-tive, and dapper with verbal innovation—suggested possibilities to other artists: most immediately to the Beatles and other '60s counterculturists, and later (to name a handful of heirs) to neotraditionalists like Williams and Tracy Chapman, confessionalists like Joni Mitchell, and shrapnel surrealists like Beck.

That lyrical and new musical style crystallized on the three albums that mark his creative peak: *Bring-ing It All Back Home*, *Highway 61 Revisited*, and *Blonde on Blonde*. Bringing the influence of all his forefathers (Hank Williams, Robert Johnson, Little Richard) to bear, he forged an all-American noise ri-valed only by Chuck Berry's. The six-minute sneer of "Like a Rolling Stone" made long songs safe for radio; the moan of "Sad Eyed Lady of the Lowlands" made for perhaps the loveliest ballad ever.

Subsequently, he's made reincarnation itself look like an art as the schooled roots-rocker of *The Base-ment Tapes*...as the creator of landmark country rock...as the melancholy exile of 1975's *Blood on the Tracks*...as an evangelizing born-again Chris-tian...as a born-again folkie...as the triumphant wise man of 1997's loamy *Time Out of Mind*.... "It doesn't matter whether it's folk, country, blues, or rock," says Williams. "It's just Bob Dylan." No one genre of American music can define Dylan, but he defines American music. —TROY PATTERSON

bob
Dylan

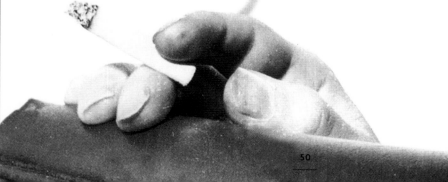

11

marlon

Brando

DELIA SALVI KNOWS WHAT'S GOING TO HAPPEN EVERY TIME SHE pulls out the dusty reel of old movie clips for a new crop of students in her directing and acting classes at UCLA. A lot of these wannabes have grown up on Brad Pitt and Julia Roberts, on acting as winks and nods and too-perfect quips, and on the marketing of celebrity. Their frame of reference begins with Tarantino and ends with *The Blair Witch Project*.

In other words, they know next to nothing.

So Salvi turns on her time machine, taking them back to Elia Kazan's *A Streetcar Named Desire* (1951) and *On the Waterfront* (1954).

To Brando.

"They flip out when they see him," says Salvi. "It fills them with awe."

Of course it does. Movie acting has gone the way of the space program, with lots of easily forgettable performances. It's hard to comprehend that man once walked on the moon.

In a half century of film, no actor—certainly no American actor—can touch Marlon Brando, although many have tried to eat off his plate. As Brando biographer Peter Manso says, "You can't even count the number of young s---s who would pay 25 bucks to watch Marlon walk across the street today."

You always knew, watching Brando fill the screen as working-class hero or ruthless Mafia don or walrus-like sexual predator, that he had opened the door to a world beyond mere performance or role-playing. Not that Pacino and Hoffman in their day, and Edward Norton, Johnny Depp, and Sean Penn today, haven't all had at least a glimmer of the understanding Brando had. But it's just that—a glimmer. Only De Niro approaches a screenplay in a similar way, as nothing but a set of clues, a treasure-hunt map in a search for the truth of a character. Brando's own demons edited whatever script he was handed, and Brando, who understood that character is everything, gave life to doomed, dangerous, fatally flawed men.

"In front of a camera or on stage, he knows. He just knows!" says Manso, who can only explain it through Greek philosophy. "He's in touch with Logos in some crazy-ass genius way."

Tragically insecure and supremely confident. Brutally macho and insufferably sensitive. Burning with ideas and incapable of eloquently articulating them. He called Hollywood a town of sellout whores, then took odd roles in trash movies, admitting it was for the money. He craved respect and shunned awards, sending a Native American woman to answer the call for his *Godfather* Oscar in 1973, thereby telling the industry to shove it.

His *Godfather* performance, hailed as the second coming, was followed up by an even more stunning turn in Bernardo Bertolucci's *Last Tango in Paris*, which not only brought a new intellectual sophistication to sex in cinema but also gave hope to fat bald guys the world over. Today, at 76, he exists almost completely out of public view, as would any self-respecting soul whose last movie of note was *The Island of Dr. Moreau* (1996).

Attempts to break this all down, to reduce Brando to some cliché of pop psychology, are sheer folly, says Manso, who spent seven years studying him. "He is a genius as an actor and a monster as a man," but a monster in the sense that the son of two alcoholics "is deeply troubled" and "carries around bags and bags of pain."

Pain that, within the safety of a character, could get boiled down to incredible vulnerability. "You could almost put your hand inside him when he was tender," Elia Kazan said in the book *The Master Director Discusses His Films*.

"My God, look at *Streetcar*," says Eva Marie Saint, who costarred with Brando three years later in *Waterfront*, for which they both won Oscars. "I mean, he was a powerhouse."

Manso says he once got a message from Anthony Hopkins, who had read his book and wondered how Brando could walk away from that talent. Manso answered that the actor discovered "there's an aspect that goes beyond talent, morality, and politics. It's character, and there's something missing in Marlon's."

And so Brando dumped on his own great art, and on Hollywood, moved to a Tahitian atoll, and continued marching to his own angry anthems. But like so many before and after him, he made the mistake of assuming that any of us care what an actor—even a brilliant one—thinks about the issues of the day. A 1996 interview on *Larry King Live*—ostensibly about violence, though it was never clear—ended up looking like Albert Brooks' take on celebrity night at an old folks' home.

King: But what…what…the essence of the message is what?

Brando: The essence of what message?

King: Your message.

Brando: I don't have a message. I am not a messenger.

King: But you have thoughts.

Brando: Yes, I do.

Save them, Marlon. Your gift to the world was Terry Malloy, Stanley Kowalski, Don Corleone, Emiliano Zapata, and a dozen others. If it's politics you want us to remember you by, we'll take the motorcycle tough in *The Wild One*. Asked what he's rebelling against, the dark-eyed lug says, "Whadda ya got?" —STEVE LOPEZ

SIMPLY THE BEST	**A STREETCAR NAMED DESIRE** (1951)	**ON THE WATER-FRONT** (1954)	**THE GODFATHER** (1972)	**LAST TANGO IN PARIS** (1973)	**THE FRESHMAN** (1990)
	As Stanley Kowalski, Brando redefined acting and inspired thousands of careers.	A sinner becomes a saint, yielding scene after classic scene.	The most one man has ever made out stuffing his cheeks.	His last masterful performance was as a despairing soul looking for redemption in debasement.	Brando proved he could laugh at himself with this charming send-up of his *Godfather* persona.

BARBRA STREISAND'S REP FOR DEMANDING CONtrol of all details related to the business of being Barbra threatens at times to become as big a headline as Barbra's rep for knocking audiences off their feet each time she opens her throat in song. Her every move may be, as Mike Myers' ultra-yenta invention Linda Richman says, "like buttah," but the singer-actor-director-producer is also like a diva: She wants quote approval. She wants photo approval. Don't get disgruntled employees started on La Streisand.

But who's more entitled to rule her universe? From the time she was a scrawny kid, astounding her showbiz elders first with her inimitable look and then with her inimitable voice, the ugly-duckling-turned-swan who used to spell her name Barbara-with-an-*a* has had to fight to make room for her unique brand, shape, and size of stardom. In the beginning, no one had heard a sound like hers. No one had seen a face like hers that hadn't been pinched and refitted to conform to blander, less ethnic standards of beauty. No one had seen a Jewish woman make such loud and proud use of her Jewishness—maybe not since Fanny Brice, the comedienne the then-21-year-old Streisand played in her career-rocketing 1964 turn on Broadway in *Funny Girl*. "You always hope that you're making something worthwhile, but you never see it as a classic while it is happening," recalls veteran producer Ray Stark—Brice's son-in-law himself—who fought the

studio to cast Streisand in the film version of *Girl*, which cemented her movie-star status and won her an Oscar. (That year, columnist Liz Smith merely called her "the greatest talent anywhere.")

Even long after the beginning, after *Hello, Dolly!* and *The Way We Were*, after her albums sold millions, after glossy mags regularly celebrated her idiosyncratic beauty, she fought: for her right to direct, to speak out on political issues, to keep her nails long—beauty trends be damned! Streisand's celebrity encapsulates, in its defiant way, all the battles and achievements of women artists in the second half of the 20th century—and yet still she struggles with stage fright. With feelings of insecurity. With a media obsessed with every detail of her life, from the homes she owns to her relationships with second husband James Brolin and Jason Gould, her 33-year-old son by first husband Elliott Gould. She even fights for the opportunity to get a good film role. "Directors [think] I'll tell them what to do," she says. "Don't they realize what a pleasure it would be not to have to care about all the details?"

Years ago, critic Rex Reed proclaimed, "Every age has its Super Lady...Sarah Bernhardt...Gertrude Lawrence...Judy Garland. Well, we've got ours. Her name is Barbra." And if being a Super Lady means sweating the details—and making those around her sweat them, too—well, who would dare say the effort isn't worth it to let Barbra be Barbra? —LS

13

barbra
Streisand

alfred Hitchcock

A HITCHCOCK FILM. TWENTY-FOUR YEARS AFTER he directed his last movie, those words still have a life of their own, conveying queasy terror, the darkest humor, and hair-raising narrative force. "I'll tell you *exactly* why my father's work endures," says Patricia Hitchcock O'Connell. "Because he made his pictures for the audience, he didn't make them for the critics. And basically audiences do not change."

It's not that simple, of course. A brilliant technical innovator steeped in old-school expressionist traditions, Alfred Hitchcock made movies that have spawned reams of modernist (and postmodernist) theory, inspired everyone from meticulous craftsman Martin Scorsese to slavish devotee Brian De Palma, and even seduced Gus Van Sant, one of the hippest directors of the '90s, to attempt (foolishly) a shot-by-shot remake of Hitchcock's masterwork *Psycho*. "He combined amazing technical ability and psychological investigation with a certain glee," explains director Atom Egoyan (*The Sweet Hereafter*). "To a filmmaker, that's an incredibly potent mix."

True enough, but daughter Patricia's pithy assessment of her father's canon is, in the end, his real legacy: At heart, movies are populist entertainment, and few understood that better than Hitch. His films—particularly those after he joined the Hollywood studio system—are stylish, profound, poetic... but always accessible. And so he populated his work with a glittering galaxy of stars who could not only draw the masses but also surrender themselves to his disturbing, feverish vision. Imagine: He transformed affable Everyman Jimmy Stewart into an obsessed voyeur (*Rear Window*), and suave matinee idol Cary Grant into a cowering, paranoid fugitive (*North by Northwest*). And that's to say nothing of the perversities inflicted upon the blond goddesses who were *his* obsession—Grace Kelly, Janet Leigh, Kim Novak, and Tippi Hedren.

In 1955, Hitchcock even embraced that most democratic of media, television. The tube would make him a brand name, and, for the first time in film history, ordinary people got to know the face behind the camera. They invited Hitch into their homes, enabling him to lure an even bigger audience into theaters and introduce them to his latter-day work—dark, weird, groundbreaking stuff that would inexorably alter the course of pop culture: the endlessly studied shower scene in *Psycho*; the wordless nine-minute sequence where Stewart tails Novak in *Vertigo*; all of *Rear Window*—which, despite its trappings of suspense, is actually a movie about...watching.

"Even more than the story and technical innovations, Hitchcock was able to put into the mainstream notions of perversity and subversive ideas," adds Egoyan, noting the early appearance of openly adulterous characters in movies like 1951's *Strangers on a Train*. "I can't even imagine what audiences during that period thought of them."

And that's exactly it. At the end of the day, it was Hitch's winking willingness to lead us by the hand into unspoken corners of American life that charged his films. That dark, macabre place where murderous conspiracies abound, birds peck men to pieces, and pristine showers are sullied with bright, slick blood, spiraling slowly down the drain. —DANIEL FIERMAN

15 ^{the} Rolling Sto

THEIR GREAT THEME IS SEX. TO BE PRECISE, THEIR GREAT THEME is shagging. Consider that the Stones' biggest hits are the bleary conquest yarn "Honky Tonk Women," the hormone-stoked "(I Can't Get No) Satisfaction," and the paradoxical bondage fantasy "Brown Sugar." Consider the objectifying "Some Girls" and a dozen other tunes unfit for explication in a family magazine. When they call themselves the World's Greatest Rock & Roll Band, they're not just boasting of their rare, rude noise. They also leeringly mean rock & roll as a synonym for intercourse, its sense in blues vernacular.

From 1963, when they issued their first single (Chuck Berry's "Come On"), such lewdness abetted the band's definitive PR stroke of playing Id to the Fab Four's Ego. As Vernon Reid, whose band Living Colour opened for the Stones in '89, says, "When the Beatles were into peace, love, and whatever, [the Stones] were doing 'Sympathy for the Devil.'" In the mid-'60s, the bouncy, Merseybeat Beatles wanted to hold your hand; the Stones—whose name comes from a swaggering Muddy Waters song—wanted you under their thumb.

By the release of the wryly sinister *Beggars Banquet* ('68), the Stones' surliness had evolved from a stunt into a viable artistic style. When they countered *Let It Be* with *Let It Bleed*, their diabolical image proved a magnet for blame when a man was killed during their set at the Altamont music festival. "By now I look upon [Altamont] as part of that era," Keith Richards told EW in 1999. "There was a lot of freedom going about, and the war. There was a lawlessness I found interesting, but it did result in some mad guy getting done."

Such a distanced outlook makes the Stones look like aesthetes, which they are. Their claim to greatness is their abstract genius with rhythm: Drummer Charlie Watts, 59, and (ex-)bassist Bill Wyman, 63, shoot straight for the hips. Brian Jones added exotic tones (the stinging sitar of "Paint It Black") before quitting the band a month prior to his '69 drowning death. His replacements on guitar (Mick Taylor, 52, through '74 and Ron Wood, 53, since) are expert journeymen—always competent, sometimes wise. Richards, 56, is the rare guitar legend worshiped not for virtuosity but for intensity, for shattering riffs like those of "Jumpin' Jack Flash." As for Mick Jagger—56 and still, we gather from the tabloids, unsatisfied—his legacy lies in bracing lyrics, bawdy delivery, and an unmatched persona: the androgynous posturing that foreran glam, the insolent snarling that prefigured punk, the self-ironic jiving that informs how current white acts (the Beastie Boys, PJ Harvey, Kid Rock, and everybody else) style their appropriations of black music.

In short, the Stones—white British bohemians whose medium is black American folk art—became World Greats by reaching across the Atlantic to amplify blues music. "I tip my hat to 'em," Muddy Waters once said. "It took the people from England to hip my people—my white people—to what they had in their own backyard." Their '74 hit to the contrary, it's not only rock & roll. At any rate, everyone likes it. —TP

audrey
Hepburn

16

HERE'S HOW A 1953 PARAMOUNT PRESS RELEASE described its newest star, Audrey Hepburn: "Completely captivating, a delightful gamin, beguiling, hoydenish, disarming, sensitive, alluring, saintlike, coquettish, [and] talented."

We'd like to add one more adjective: tough-as-nails.

Consider the time *Breakfast at Tiffany's*—the 1961 classic in which Hepburn croons Henry Mancini's sentimental ballad "Moon River"—was screened for the head of the studio. "At the end of the preview, he said, 'I can tell you one thing,'" remembers director Blake Edwards. "'We've got to get rid of that f---ing song.' And Audrey said, 'Over my dead body.'"

The story is classic Hepburn, and it contains the secret to her allure: Behind her daintiness lurked an iron determination; behind her modesty, conviction; and behind her warmth, a quiet reserve. As Shirley MacLaine, her costar in *The Children's Hour* (1961), remarked when Hepburn died, "If there was a cross between the salt of the earth and a regal queen, then she was it."

The delightful Hepburn paradox made itself known from the start, with her Oscar-winning American debut in *Roman Holiday* (1953). One minute, she's a gal zipping around Italian streets on a motor scooter with prole Gregory Peck, the next she's an ultra-formal princess at a press conference. And so it remained throughout her career—a giddy yet tenacious girl in love in *Sabrina* (1954), a guttersnipe with a noble soul in *My Fair Lady* (1964), a smothered but proudly self-sufficient wife in *Two for the Road* (1967).

"In Audrey, there was a fragility which was also a strength," says screenwriter Frederic Raphael, who penned *Road*. "Audrey had had a number of experiences that were seriously traumatic, and she was marred by that, but you couldn't see the mark."

Among those traumatic experiences: her childhood in Nazi-occupied Holland. Though born to pampered aristocracy in 1929 (she was the daughter of a Dutch baroness), the young Hepburn endured the murder of relatives, survived on eating tulip bulbs, and carried secret messages for the Resistance in her ballet shoes.

After that, no doubt, the bullies in show business must have seemed like no big deal.

Hepburn's reign in Hollywood was surprisingly short—just 15 years. After 1967's *Wait Until Dark* (which proved that her delicate beauty also encased a versatile, surprisingly rich and sophisticated acting talent), Hepburn made only sporadic appearances on screen before cancer took her life in 1993. But 30 years after her cinema heyday, she exerts undiminished influence. Hepburn's innate grace and elegance, her slender silhouette—appearing as it did in the voluptuous-fleshpot-and-bleach-blond era of Monroe and Mansfield—virtually invented the archetype still found in the pages of today's fashion magazines. Look at any young actress gliding down the Oscar runway in a designer gown, and the truth becomes clear: There is only one woman they dream of being. Billy Wilder, who directed her in *Sabrina*, said it best: "After so many drive-in waitresses, here is class." —AJJ

PHOTOGRAPH BY PHILIPPE HALSMAN

SIMPLY THE BEST

ROMAN HOLIDAY (1953)

An Oscar for her first leading role, as a runaway princess charmed by reporter Gregory Peck

FUNNY FACE (1957)

Her beatnik-turned-model is s'wonderful, especially when she and Fred Astaire engage in a romantic pas de deux in Paris.

BREAKFAST AT TIFFANY'S (1961)

A gloss on Capote's original novel, but Hepburn is heartbreaking as Manhattan party girl Holly Golightly.

▲ *MY FAIR LADY* (1964)

Even if that's Marni Nixon's voice when Hepburn opens her mouth to sing, the star's Eliza Doolittle is lovely.

ROBIN AND MARIAN (1967)

Robin Hood (Sean Connery) and his maid mull over the wonders of middle-aged love in this wise romance.

john Wayne

HOW DO YOU BUILD A MYTH? THROUGH WHAT process of will, artistry, or luck did Marion Michael Morrison become John Wayne? The former was a skinny kid from Iowa who grew up in the suburbs of Los Angeles; the son of a gentle, struggling pharmacist; a man who disliked horses. The latter was, and still is, middle America's dream of itself. As the frontier faded into history during the 20th century, Wayne became the face of its remembered spirit: plainspoken, defiant, inherently nostalgic. He is the very image of our roots, and that is why, at the turn of the millennium, in the age of the Internet's shadowy come-ons, he remains the only movie star that matters to many people.

How did he do it? In part, from honing his craft in near invisibility. Throughout the 1930s, Wayne toiled in low-rent Westerns, learning the tricks of riding and prairie bearing from mentors like stuntman Yakima Canutt. But the true makeover was the actor's, and it was conscious. "When I started, I knew I was no actor, and I went to work on the Wayne thing," he said late in life. "It was as deliberate a projection as you'll ever see.... I practiced in front of a mirror."

So it was that when John Ford came calling with the role of the Ringo Kid in 1939's *Stagecoach*, John Wayne was truly born, gliding before a vast rear-projection vista like Venus on the half saddle. He rose to his full power, however, during the postwar years, when he became both the period's No. 1 box office attraction and a visual correlative to Cold War American strength.

Is that an odd development for a career-minded man who spent WWII nervously stalling the draft? Perhaps—and perhaps that's why Wayne's performances in classics like *Red River* (1948), *Sands of Iwo Jima* (1949), John Ford's 1948–50 "cavalry trilogy," and *The Searchers* (1956) are far more complicated than either his devotees or detractors allow (his Oscar-winning turn as Rooster Cogburn in 1969's *True Grit* is simple—and simply enjoyable—by comparison). In particular, as *The Searchers*' racist, vengeance-consumed Ethan Edwards, Wayne explicitly portrays the kind of brutal man who made the West safe for civilization, and thus had to be left behind by it. It's a performance marked by insight, craft, and a refusal to prettify, and it gives the lie to the alternative myth that grew up around "John Wayne" in the 1960s—that he was a simpleminded cowboy reactionary.

No, the man was an actor—just one with a persona so self-contained that unlike Marlon Brando or Gary Cooper, he has no imitators among today's performers. There is no school of Wayne, and there needn't be. Not when his image is strong enough to be digitized into a 1990s beer ad—and big enough to serve as a metaphor for a whole culture. Wayne often cited an old Mexican saying as his unofficial epitaph: *Feo, fuerte, y formal*— "He was ugly, he was strong, he had dignity." Clearly, that's how he saw the country he came to embody as well. —TY BURR

17

elizabeth
Taylor

DURING ELIZABETH TAYLOR'S EARLY DAYS AT METRO-Goldwyn-Mayer, studio execs wanted to pluck her thick eyebrows, lighten her raven hair to brown, and change her name to Virginia. But her father angrily told them they would either have to take young Elizabeth the way she was or not at all. It was a prophetic moment for the girl who not only grew up to set the standard for 20th-century beauty, style, and stardom, but who, every step of the way, lived life on her own boundless terms.

Taylor has always been a contradiction in terms, no matter what the terms are. She has been revered for over 50 years as the world's most beautiful woman, yet no public figure has been mocked more cruelly for fluctuations in her appearance. She is, even now, the definition of a movie star, though she has not starred in a feature film in two decades. She epitomizes both excess (too many jewels, marriages, pounds, ailments) and selflessness: Few entertainers mounted the barricades in the fight against AIDS with more consistency. She is someone about whom we think we know everything and yet we know very little.

We *do* know that she's a wonderful and under-rated actress. Her on-screen magic goes far deeper than those stunning violet eyes, to the raw emotions that simmer beneath her satin skin. No one has captured the pure, unconditional love that exists between humans and animals better than she did in *National Velvet* (1944), the movie that made her a star at age 12. And as frumpy, foulmouthed, alcoholic Martha in 1966's *Who's Afraid of Virginia Woolf?*, for which she earned the second of her two Best Actress Oscars, she delivered a textured performance, at once sensual and spiteful. Taylor continued making hits through the '60s, playing a wide

range of parts—from *Cleopatra* ('63), for which she received an unprecedented $1 million, to a pricey prostitute in *Butterfield 8* ('60), an Oscar-winning gig in which she made a white slip and a fur coat the sauciest ensemble imaginable. Watch her in anything, in fact, and you'll understand that overused adjective *magnetic*—Taylor quite literally draws all eyes to her whenever she's on screen.

And when she's off. Taylor's life has been a Hollywood epic, an entrancing soap opera spun across six decades, eight marriages, and 55 movies and laced with the kind of tragic and romantic turns Hollywood often promises but rarely delivers. "I've been through it all, baby," she once said. "I'm Mother Courage." A child star packaged by the Hollywood studio system and raised in an era when sexuality on the screen was suppressed, Taylor was also one of the first women to rip apart the saintly studio image. Her scandalous affair with Richard Burton, while she was married to Eddie Fisher, with whom she had had an affair while he was married to her friend Debbie Reynolds, prompted the Vatican to deem her "a woman of loose morals."

Of course, that seductive image was later softened by a string of battles—with drug and booze addictions, hip surgeries, a brain tumor, obesity, and love—which turned her instead into our favorite survivor. Through it all, she's stood stoically, facing fear and fabulousness at once, flouting and thus redefining every expectation of how she's supposed to behave. "I tease her," says good friend Rod Steiger, "that somebody somewhere created the largest voodoo doll ever and it looks like her. She laughs, but it's true. She has this quiet resolve. She's the definition of the non-quitter and the ultimate humanist." —BETTY CORTINA

▲ *NATIONAL VELVET* (1944)
Preternaturally poised and impassioned as an adolescent equestrienne who comes in first in the Grand National

A PLACE IN THE SUN (1951)
Taylor's a figure of unbearable, remote beauty in this adaptation of Dreiser's *An American Tragedy*.

▲ *CAT ON A HOT TIN ROOF* (1958)
A peerless Tennessee Williams heroine, Taylor's Maggie rails at fate and wimpy men.

BUTTERFIELD 8 (1960)
Her first Oscar, for playing a high-priced call girl. A great performance in a not-so-great movie.

WHO'S AFRAID OF VIRGINIA WOOLF? (1966)
Taylor and Burton blistered the screen as Edward Albee's battling George and Martha. Liz won another Oscar, too.

SIMPLY THE BEST

I NEVER LOVED A MAN THE WAY I LOVE YOU (1967)
Her gospel-fueled album, the first of many collaborations with producer Jerry Wexler, took Aretha to the top of the R&B charts for the first time. Featured such memorable tunes as "Dr. Feelgood," "Do Right Woman–Do Right Man," and "Drown in My Own Tears."

"RESPECT" (1967)
The roof-raising, sock-it-to-you single became an anthem for the burgeoning feminist movement.

"THINK" (1968)
Self-assured, forceful, and impossibly funky, "Think" helped Aretha claim the title of Queen of Soul.

PHOTOGRAPHS BY LEE FRIEDLANDER

aretha
Franklin

THE EVERYDAY WORLD NEVER SEEMS TO STAND IN ARETHA Franklin's way. You can hear it at the end of "Dr. Feelgood." The Queen of Soul may be singing about sexual satisfaction, but her spirit is on a *higher* plane. How else could she break up the word *good* into a soul-stirring 12-syllable benediction, as in "Great God Almighty! That man sure makes me feel go-o-o-o-o-o-od!"

Like so much of what Aretha has recorded over the past 40 years, "Feelgood" is pure revelation. Her longtime Atlantic Records producer Jerry Wexler noticed that otherworldly quality on an early recording; someone had documented the then 13-year-old singing in the Detroit Baptist church presided over by her father, Rev. Clarence L. Franklin. "It was celestial! Cosmic!" Wexler says. "It was heaven expressing itself in human form."

He eventually signed her in 1966, when she was 24. What followed was a string of gospel-fueled, full-throttle hits— "A Natural Woman," "Respect," "Chain of Fools," "Think"— all of which helped articulate a burgeoning genre called soul, and came about as close as pop culture can to divine communion. "She's infused with a spirit bigger than you and me, and that's why people respond to her," says David Ritz, who co-wrote Franklin's autobiography, *Aretha: From These Roots.* "When she gets to the essence of her music, to a gospel place,

something happens that's both mystery and magic."

The first woman inducted into the Rock and Roll Hall of Fame has worked her mojo on the public (amassing 20 No. 1 R&B hits), the music industry (15 Grammys), Kings (Martin Luther Jr.), and Queens (Elizabeth II). She's had high times (playing at President Clinton's '92 inauguration) and lows: Franklin's beloved father died in '84 from gunshot wounds suffered during a burglary. She's weathered several stormy relationships. And in the '80s, Aretha was a victim, some say, of mediocre material and management more keen on cashing in on trends than on honing a national treasure's unbridled spirit.

But at the start of a new century, Aretha's resurgent again. By sticking with the bluesy, earthy, grown-up emotionalism that took her to prominence, she's survived disco, house, rap, techno, and Britney Spears to show, as Ritz claims, "she's the 20th century's greatest vocalist." In 1998, she had a big hit with the Lauryn Hill-penned "A Rose Is Still a Rose," and she proved to be the undisputed heavyweight among VH1's class of '98 Divas. "Aretha isn't like other singers," says collaborator Luther Vandross. "You don't need her highest note to understand her greatness; she's as good in neutral. Every note, every nuance is an entire story." Amen. —DAVID HOCHMAN

LADY SOUL (1968)
Classic '60s Aretha, with its overflowing emotion, boundless energy, and unquenchable spirit on singles like "Chain of Fools," "A Natural Woman," "Since You've Been Gone (Sweet Sweet Baby)," and "People Get Ready"

"A ROSE IS STILL A ROSE" (1998)
Written and produced by multiple Grammy winner Lauryn Hill, the sultry single introduced the soulful diva to a whole new generation of Aretha-loving hip swivelers.

ROBERT DE NIRO'S PARANOID DIATRIBE FROM *Taxi Driver*—"You talkin' to me? You talkin' to *me*?!"—has turned into a scrap of pop-culture boilerplate by now. It's a slogan; you see it on T-shirts. Frat boys blurt it out after too many beers. Ironically, though, the magnificence of Robert De Niro's acting has very little to do with showy verbal eruptions: His most magnetic scenes suck you in at that savage moment when nobody's talkin' at all. In his book *Monster*, John Gregory Dunne remembers pruning the script for 1981's *True Confessions* with his wife and writing partner, Joan Didion. Great actors "create mystery by leaving things unsaid," Dunne writes. "In our screenplay of my novel *True Confessions*, Robert De Niro, who played a Catholic monsignor with a taste for the better things in life, wanted his lines pared to the minimum; his only specific request was that we write him a scene without a single word of dialogue."

De Niro hates doing interviews; he dislikes small talk. Instead he communicates with his limbs, his knees, his fingers, his belly, his grin, his pupils, his fists, his neck, that weird mole on his cheek; as the young Vito Corleone in *The Godfather Part II*, he speaks volumes with the simple, slow nod of his chin. Yes, De Niro voyaged to Italy to absorb a local dialect for *Godfather II*—a film in which he utters only 17 words of English—but it's his physical movements that pulse like omens of the man Vito Corleone will eventually become: the aging Don played by Marlon Brando. "His gesture as he refuses the gift of a box of groceries is beautifully expressive and has the added wonder of suggesting Brando, and not from the outside but from the inside," critic Pauline Kael marveled in 1974. "Even the soft, cracked Brando-like voice seems to come from the inside.... De Niro is right to be playing the young Brando because he has the physical audacity, the grace, and the instinct to become a great actor—perhaps as great as Brando."

We know now, 26 years later, that De Niro has climbed to those heights; he's done it not by sculpting a fixed movie-star identity, but by keeping his body in constant flux. De Niro was a skittering bundle of nerves as Johnny Boy, the cherry-bomb hooligan in 1973's *Mean Streets*; he dropped his muscles into deep freeze as the catatonic Leonard in 1990's *Awakenings*; he slipped into an armor of sinew and skin art as a skeezy ex-con in 1991's *Cape Fear*. And most famously, he toned into fighting trim—and then let his body crash and burn into blubbery gluttony—as boxer Jake La Motta in 1980's *Raging Bull*, the most furious aria in the actor's ongoing opera of duets with director Martin Scorsese. "Marlon Brando changed acting when he walked across the stage in *A Streetcar Named Desire*," says Chazz Palminteri, who sparred with De Niro in 1993's *A Bronx Tale*. "De Niro changed it with *Raging Bull*. At that time, no actors transformed themselves the way he did. They do it now. But they do it because of him." Talking? Hell, when Robert De Niro *walks*, people listen. —BC

robert
DeNiro

the global
Star Map

IF HE HADN'T BEEN INFLUENCED BY THE FLICKERING majesty of Ingmar Bergman and Federico Fellini, Woody Allen might still be doing stand-up. If it weren't for the electronic example of Kraftwerk, the human beat box might still provide backing for rap. And without the immaculate beauty of Catherine Deneuve, Earth would surely be a duller planet. Here's a polyglot rider to our exclusively Anglophone list—a tip of the chapeau to some preeminent global villagers. —TP

SPAIN

PEDRO ALMODOVAR Maybe the funniest director of the last 20 years. His best film— *Women on the Verge of a Nervous Breakdown*—is part melodrama, part farce, all crazily candy-colored. There's also more than a bit of his high-screwball sensibility in indies like *The Opposite of Sex.*

ITALY

SOPHIA LOREN The only actress to win an Oscar for a foreign-language film (for her leading role in *Two Women*), she's a movie queen, a saucy comedian (see *Marriage Italian Style*), and our earthiest sex symbol.

LUIS BUNUEL Four decades after unleashing surrealism on cinema with *Un Chien Andalou*, Buñuel raised it to the sly sublime with *Belle de Jour* and *That Obscure Object of Desire.*

FEDERICO FELLINI Music videos and TV ads reference the flamboyant fantasies of *8½*, but it's his neorealist parables (*La Strada, Nights of Cabiria*) and the introspective, irreplaceable *La Dolce Vita* that will age best.

MARCELLO MASTROIANNI The epitome of modern melancholy in *La Dolce Vita* and *8½*, easily wry in a range of sex comedies, he was both an apathetic sad sack and the ideal Latin lover.

PAKISTAN

NUSRAT FATEH ALI KHAN The legendary qawwali singer's 1997 death came just as disparate admirers (Eddie Vedder, Peter Gabriel, Massive Attack) were helping him find a larger audience.

INDIA

RAVI SHANKAR Hear the haunting strings on the Beatles' "Within You Without You"? It was Shankar who opened Western ears to Eastern music by introducing pop stars to the sitar.

SATYAJIT RAY The recipient of an Oscar for "his profound humanitarian outlook." His atmospheric lyricism is best realized in the *Apu* trilogy, an epic that puts him on a par with Jean Renoir, Bergman, and Kurosawa.

LUCIANO PAVAROTTI He became opera's equivalent of a rock superstar and, along with Placido Domingo and José Carreras (together they are best known as the Three Tenors), brought his art to a pop audience on an unprecedented scale.

NIGERIA

FELA ANIKULAPO KUTI The most original artist shelved under the world-beat rubric. His postcolonial party music depended on a give-and-take with funk and soul.

FRANCE

CATHERINE DENEUVE An icy princess most commanding when hysteria sullies her elegance (see *Repulsion, Belle de Jour, Indochine*).

JEAN-PAUL BELMONDO The actor's unconventional looks—boxer's nose, ropelike lips—personified the French new wave's antihero hunk, particularly in the film *Breathless*. Every current Bogart wannabe works in Belmondo's shadow, too.

JEANNE MOREAU Moreau—in *Les Amants*, in *La Notte*, in *Jules and Jim*—established herself as the doyenne of art cinema, showing America that intelligence could be just as seductive as glamour.

JEAN-LUC GODARD The subject of his films is film. So *Breathless*, new wave's signature work, is an essay on crime thrillers. Any wonder Quentin Tarantino's production company is named after the analytical gangster flick *Bande à Part*?

ROBERT BRESSON The best of his austere, painterly masterworks—*Pickpocket, Mouchette, Au Hasard Balthazar*—shaped the work of movie existentialists from Truffaut to Martin Scorsese.

SERGE GAINSBOURG Creator of the internationally scandalous "Je T'Aime...Moi Non Plus," he remains an alt-rock idol for his lush arrangements and louche antics.

BRIGITTE BARDOT Made famous by Roger Vadim (*And... God Created Woman*) and deconstructed by Godard (*Contempt*), BB could pout like a pneumatic nymphet—her nearly illicit sensuality made her the epitome of the Euro bombshell.

FRANÇOIS TRUFFAUT A truant, a critic, a true man of cinema. His exuberant masterworks—*The 400 Blows, Jules and Jim, Day for Night*—exude a pure movie love that has infected directors as commercial as Steven Spielberg, who cast Truffaut in *Close Encounters of the Third Kind*.

JOHN WOO Purveyor of the most glamorous violence this side of *The Wild Bunch*, Woo—in films from Hong Kong's *Hard-Boiled* to Hollywood's *Face/Off*—makes a gunfight move like a minuet.

HONG HONG

BRUCE LEE Compact, dynamic, consistently thrilling, the kung fu king was born in the U.S., made his mark in Hong Kong, and with *Enter the Dragon*, popularized martial arts films the world over.

CHINA

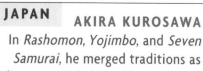

ZHANG YIMOU AND GONG LI
In color-saturated historical dramas (*Raise the Red Lantern, Ju Dou*), China's best director teamed with its most luminous star to confront their country's history and indulge a uniquely ravishing richness of style.

JAPAN

AKIRA KUROSAWA
In *Rashomon, Yojimbo*, and *Seven Samurai*, he merged traditions as diverse as Kabuki and horse opera, inspiring everything from spaghetti Westerns to *Star Wars*.

GERMANY

KRAFTWERK By pioneering the synthetic soundscapes that undergird hip-hop and electronica, they proved to be the first band of the 21st century, way back in the '70s.

WERNER HERZOG Master of the grand grotesque, Herzog makes films (*Fitzcarraldo; Aguirre, the Wrath of God*) hypnotic to watch and hard to forget, especially for punkish auteurs like Harmony Korine.

SWEDEN

INGMAR BERGMAN
The bleak *Seventh Seal* and touchingly intimate *Wild Strawberries* were at the forefront of our late-'50s art-house movement and enjoy a continual revival in the minds of self-made philosophers like Woody Allen.

ABBA The definitive Europop act—cheerfully bland, irresistibly groovy. At one point, the quartet sold more albums worldwide than any other group and, by the end of the '70s, bested Volvo as Sweden's top export.

stephen King

IT FIGURES AMERICA'S REIGNING KING OF HORROR would have a sick sense of humor. Flashing you with a mouthful of chewed food is one of Stephen King's favorite gags. So are dead-baby jokes. "Actually, he can be very funny," says friend and fellow scribe Peter Straub (*Ghost Story*). "In conversation, Steve can make you laugh until your sides hurt."

On paper, King slays, too. By last count, well more than 225 million copies of his 49 books, have been sold, making him one of the world's best-selling authors—though he'd be the first to tell you that such a record has little to do with exceptional prose: He's summed up his propulsive, plot-driven novels as "the literary equivalent of a Big Mac and large fries," and doubts he'll "ever be remembered as a literary giant." That assessment irks one of his biggest fans, Frank Darabont, the director responsible for 2 of the 27 movie adaptations of King stories ("Rita Hayworth and the Shawshank Redemption" and *The Green Mile*). "His ability to spin a good yarn is the very thing critics seem to disdain. You know what? The critics said the same damn thing about Charles Dickens."

In truth, subscribing to the King-is-trashy-fun-but-not-real-literature school of thought is a bit clichéd at this point. Critics do take him seriously now; his later novels (*Misery, Dolores Claiborne*) in particular have resonance and depth—in addition to scaring the pants off you. Says Darabont, "He creates people and worlds so rich, experiencing one of his stories feels like having a full meal."

King began hammering horror on an Underwood typewriter as a teen, inspired by the likes of author Richard Matheson, whose *I Am Legend* showed him that your own backyard can yield enough sinister material for any novelist. Said King in 1977: "I think my greatest fear is...fear of what I might do in any given situation." Such gutsy honesty has imbued his horror with a moving humanity. "That he has something like a genius for tightening the narrative screws wouldn't mean half as much if he did not also have such extraordinary sympathy for the people he has arrayed on stage," says Straub.

While nuclear families frequently implode in his fiction, King's own home life is his saving grace. It was his wife, Tabitha (also a novelist), who pulled his novel *Carrie* out of the trash, and he's often remarked upon the sanity of his cloistered Maine lifestyle. Certainly it has permitted him to create a body of work the notably prodigious Dickens would have admired. (To avoid glutting the market, King wrote six books under the pseudonym Richard Bachman.) Even the recent car accident that affected his mobility doesn't seem to have slowed his literary output; if anything, we might expect an even freer flow of works to emerge in the wake of this true-life nightmare. And King, 52, has said he will stop only when he's out of ideas—a day his idol hopes will never dawn. "He's a great storyteller," says Richard Matheson. "And he's getting better and better." —JEFF JENSEN

21

mary
Tyler Moore

GIGGLING AT THE FUNERAL OF CHUCKLES THE Clown, misfiring with every dinner party, suffering the Happy Homemaker, the gruff boss, and her abrasive neighbors with the grace and humor of a good woman unwittingly *better* than those around her, Mary Richards lives on as the most fully realized character ever to inhabit a prime-time sitcom. Why? Three little words: Mary Tyler Moore. Oh, sure, Moore is quick to praise *The Mary Tyler Moore Show*'s writers and her costars. "I wanted my laughs to come out of relationships," Moore says, "the private anguishes and fears that people could relate to."

But let's be honest. The success behind America's most beloved sitcom comes down to one thing: Moore's unsurpassed comic timing. Her impeccable sixth sense made ratings lightning strike twice: First in the form of Laura Petrie on *The Dick Van Dyke Show*, in which Moore provided an insouciantly idealized version of the 1960s housewife, and in the next decade as news producer Mary Richards. For a generation of Americans, Mary was woman—strong, single, searching, silly—and she roared with a nation's growing pains. "First, she was the girl everyone fell in love with—and God knows, I was one of them," says *Mary Tyler Moore* cocreator James L. Brooks. "Then she became this icon of a new age, this independent woman. That's what's remarkable about her."

Moore's career underwent a similar trajectory: She started out as a dancing elf in an appliance commercial. After a run of dispiriting auditions, she nearly missed trying out for Laura Petrie. In a Mary Richards-esque fit of insecurity, she recalls proclaiming, "Oh, no. I can't take another disappointment, so I'm not going." But spunk prevailed, and after two Emmys and a five-year run, she was rewarded with her own show, one that would put four more Emmys on her mantel. Her success, however, didn't come without a price: She struggled to break out of Mary Richards' long shadow, though that too produced its triumphs. In 1980 she plumbed another, steelier persona with her Oscar-nominated turn as *Ordinary People*'s domineering matriarch. "It wasn't until years later that I recognized someone else in that role, and it was me," says Moore. "Aside from Mary Richards, there is another person who is darker."

Moore further skewered her image in 1996, playing a neurotic Jewish mother in David O. Russell's comedy *Flirting With Disaster*. "She knows how to use that iconography of herself," says Russell. "She uses her Mary Tyler Moore-ness to be funny and riveting in different ways." The reaches of her influence extended further when she spoke publicly of her battles with diabetes and alcoholism—brave disclosures that helped soften the stigmas of the diseases. As America's sweetheart and an animal-rights crusader (before it was cool), she looms large on our pop-cultural landscape. "I was walking down the street a few years ago and somebody yelled out, 'You're an icon!'" recalls Moore, now 63. "My husband reminded me that my 3-year-old nephew had earlier called me a doodie head. You know, it's all in the perception." —JESSICA SHAW

22

"BEFORE I WORKED WITH JACK, I WAS HAVING a drunken argument with another comedy writer about who was the best actor alive," recalls James L. Brooks, who directed Nicholson's Academy Award-winning turns in *Terms of Endearment* and *As Good as It Gets*. "I was arguing that Jack was, and I finally won my point when I said Jack could play either role in *The Odd Couple*."

What better testament to the astonishing breadth of Nicholson's talent than to imagine him as germ-phobe Felix *and* superslob Oscar? After all, he's pulled off parts as disparate as Eugene O'Neill (*Reds*) and the Joker (*Batman*). "You don't want to do one job and be dead—play one character and that's it," Nicholson told EW in 1998. "If I could've tolerated that, I would've been one of these billion-dollars-rich television actors."

The actor's wallet hardly suffered: He took home $50 million for *Batman* alone. But if not for Rip Torn, Nicholson could very well have ended up a TV staple. Torn had intended to play *Easy Rider*'s pot-smoking lawyer, but he dropped out, giving Nicholson—a then-struggling actor in guest spots (*The Andy Griffith Show*) and B flicks—the role that made him a star. (Would it have been so bad if the two *had* switched careers? Think of Nicholson as Artie on *The Larry Sanders Show*.) Nicholson's first of three Oscars came for his exhilarating performance in the mental-hospital opus *One Flew Over the Cuckoo's Nest* (1975), a role that highlights his greatest gift: the ability to bring the lightest touch to the heaviest material. "He's a very intense, focused actor who can play a powerful dramatic role and at the same time bring an ironic humor to it," says low-budget legend Roger Corman, who introduced Nicholson to movie audiences in 1958's *The Cry Baby Killer*. Adds Brooks: "Everybody senses that he gets the joke. He doesn't take himself or anything else too seriously."

Even his career. In 1975, the Neptune, N.J., native teasingly quipped that he'd reached his goal "to be considered for everything." But the truth is, despite more power than perhaps any other actor in the business, he's never turned complacent. Witness his willingness to take on such tough sells as the Depression-era character study *Ironweed* and the Sean Penn-directed downer *The Crossing Guard*. "There's a tendency when you're a star to play it safe," says Brooks. "Jack doesn't know that road."

Perhaps the best way to view Nicholson is as a bridge between old Hollywood glamour and modern-day grit. He can be as crustily charming as James Cagney ("You make me want to be a better man," he tells Helen Hunt in *As Good as It Gets*), and as cartoonishly ferocious as a WWF wrestler (his "You can't handle the truth!" rant in *A Few Good Men*). "There's a grace to him, but he's not afraid of the devil inside him," Brooks explains. "We all would like to accept ourselves like that." —BRUCE FRETTS

jack
Nicholson

SIMPLY THE BEST

I STARTED OUT AS A CHILD (1964)

This album of youthful reminiscence—a topic that would become Cosby's comic signature—snagged a Grammy award, as did his next *five* LPs.

I SPY (1965–68)

As globe-trotting agent Alexander "Scotty" Scott, Cosby won three straight Emmys.

THE BILL COSBY SHOW (1969–71)

Not since the unenlightened days of *Amos and Andy* had a black man been cast as the star of a sitcom. Rack up another trail blazed by the now-in-demand Cosby.

▲ *FAT ALBERT AND THE COSBY KIDS* (DEBUTED 1972)

Returning to his inner-city roots, he created, exec-produced, hosted, *and* supplied voices for the autobiographical Saturday-morning standby.

THE COSBY SHOW (1984–92)

With this decade-defining classic, Cosby elevated a network (the then-struggling NBC), the issue of race on TV (by largely negating it), and the sitcom (which would never be quite the same again).

bill Cosby

24

THERE'S A FAMOUS STORY ABOUT BILL COSBY—possibly even true—that after his first big payday as a stand-up comic, he celebrated by pouring the cash onto his bed and rolling around in the bills all night long.

He'd need an awfully big bed to hold the bucks he's made since then; at age 62, he's worth an estimated $400 million. Still, even putting aside his straight commercial success, Cosby can measure his cultural impact with loftier yardsticks. In the mid-'60s, he was the first black comic whose stand-up act was bought by mainstream America, with albums that regularly went gold (this at the height of the polarizing civil rights movement). Cosby's wry homilies (on everything from Noah's Ark to his childhood pals, including—"hey, hey, hey"—a kid named Fat Albert) were soon trivialized by Richard Pryor's edgier, blacker humor. But without Cosby's unparalleled crossover success, would there have been a Pryor? Certainly the first African-American star of a TV drama would have been a longer time coming: Cosby broke that col-

or barrier in 1965, when he teamed up with Robert Culp on the popular series *I Spy.*

Cosby was making history again in the '80s, this time with a sitcom of his own design that, in its color-blind presentation of its main characters, made a black family America's first family. *The Cosby Show* was so beloved (at its peak, on Thursday nights nearly half the nation's sets were tuned to Brooklyn's Huxtables), it raised NBC from the Nielsen ashes, helping to turn it into the Must See powerhouse of the '90s. "At the time, comedy was perceived to be dead and the network was terrified," remembers *Cosby Show* executive producer Tom Werner. "So what Bill did was quite daring."

How has Cosby managed to continually defy the odds? "At the end of the day," says Phylicia Rashad, who played Clair Huxtable and was Cosby's costar on his most recent CBS sitcom, *Cosby,* "Bill is about people. He looks a lot at the way people live and their concerns. And that's universal." No, that's revolutionary. —B C

IN 1963, A RISING YOUNG ACTOR WAS riding his motorcycle through Utah when, on a whim, he decided to take a cutoff through the Wasatch Mountains. He was so enchanted with the pristine landscape that he bought what few acres he could afford. As time went on, and the actor prospered, he bought more land there—and built a ski resort, which morphed into a filmmakers' retreat, which launched a revolution that helped change how movies get made, distributed, and seen in this country. Robert Redford had named his spread after one of his more popular roles, but these days the word *Sundance* has come to signify a sphere of movie creativity more vibrant than Hollywood itself.

To a lot of his fans, however, Redford's transformation in the past two decades may seem as random as that early high-canyon turnoff. Which is to say that many still think of him as not just an actor, not even as a mere star, but as *the* embodiment of the stoic-yet-sensitive, post-'60s male: the Me Generation's very own rugged matinee idol on the order of Clark Gable. The grudging flip side to this attitude is that since Redford, as a performer, is such a potent image, how are we to take his endeavors as director, mentor, and activist seriously?

Well, as he himself said in a 1974 interview, "image is crap." And since Redford has built his alternate careers with the judicious honesty that marks his best on-screen work, his performing days now look like a glorious apprenticeship for real life.

There are few movies as entertaining as *Butch Cassidy and the Sundance Kid*, *The Sting*, *The Way We Were*, or *All the President's Men*, but can anybody say they are as deeply felt or as attuned to character as *Ordinary People*, *A River Runs Through It*, and *Quiz Show*—films in which Redford does not appear but that bristle with their director's sincere, unchic intelligence?

Still, when he bothers to show up in front of a camera—Redford has starred in a mere 10 films in the last 20 years—he's a reminder of just how appealing old-school charisma can be. The actor's knack for emotional reticence was a rarity in the '70s, when many of his peers writhed in Brando-derived torment, and that watchful remove still means that a viewer's eye automatically seeks him out in any scene, even when he's slumming in a trash-TV-ready melodrama like *Indecent Proposal*. Says Sydney Pollack, who has directed Redford seven times: "In my opinion, he's one of the best movie actors we've ever had in this country.... He's never doing nothing, but he does often hold something back, which, for me, only makes him more interesting."

Perhaps it's best, then, to consider Redford's retreat from the movie-star game as the ultimate act of holding back. But is it too much to hope that the quixotic paradoxes of playing an aging sex symbol might induce him to turn, once more, onto the highway and into our view? —TB

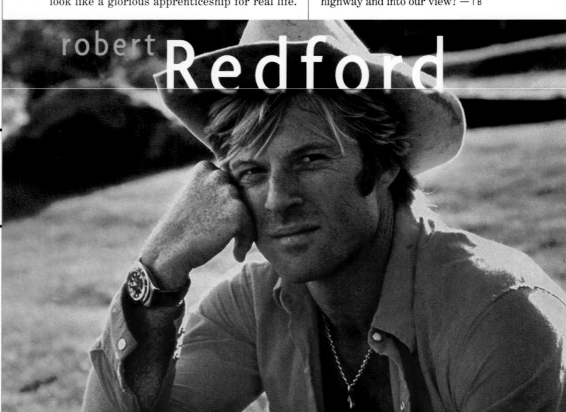

robert **Redford**

woody Allen

26

FEARLESSLY PROLIFIC, OBLIVIOUS TO TREND, AND unshakably true to his muse, Woody Allen has flourished in a Hollywood increasingly ruled by F/X bombast and almighty marketing departments. "For him, self-expression is a large part of the equation," notes longtime screenwriting partner Marshall Brickman. "He doesn't buttonhole people to ask, 'What kind of movie should I make?'"

Rather, Allen has always known what kind of movies he *needed* to make. Just as he himself has been ruled by the dueling obsessions of love and death (not coincidentally, the name of an early film), his oeuvre is indelibly stamped with a wry mixture of romance and fatalism. You can see the subtext of these twin urges in everything from period pieces celebrating his youth (*Radio Days*) to far-flung "art" projects (*Interiors*) to whimsical

fantasies (*Zelig*). And at his best, Allen can spin this Freudian dance into tragicomic odes of sweeping beauty: Has there ever been a serenade to a city more elegant than *Manhattan*? Or a ballad to a woman more romantic than *Annie Hall*?

Although the ugly complications of his personal life have cast a shadow over later work, there's no denying he created some of the finest roles for actresses (Diane Keaton, Mia Farrow). As for accusations of elitism in his narrative focus—too rich, too white—consider how rare a personal point of view is today. As Sam Waterston (*Crimes and Misdemeanors*) says: "It's not enough to figure out the system. You have to have something to say. To be able to go on and on like this and be interesting is unique." If not for Allen, impossible. —MF

clint
Eastwood

ONE COULD CALL CLINT EASTWOOD THE CONSUM-
mate cinematic politician. He played a good ol' boy
under Jimmy Carter (*Every Which Way but
Loose*); a trigger-happy lawman under Ronald Reagan (who quoted the *Sudden Impact* line "Go
ahead—make my day"); a kinder, gentler
gunslinger under George Bush (*Unforgiv-
en*); and a philanderer under Bill Clinton
(*The Bridges of Madison County*).

One could call him this, except that unlike your average politico, the onetime mayor
of Carmel, Calif., never pandered to the public.
"I don't make films with regard to the commercial
aspect," he told an interviewer in '92, citing one of
his least popular characters, a flamboyant film
director inspired by John Huston. "I'm entirely in
agreement with...John Wilson in [1990's] *White
Hunter, Black Heart*: 'I won't let 8 million popcorn
eaters pull me this way and that.'"

No, but those kernel crunchers sure followed him. A
star formed from fewer words than possibly any leading man since the silent era (to wit, his mere fistful of
lines in *A Fistful of Dollars*), Eastwood had a hoarse
whisper and emotional economy that were the blueprint for the modern action hero. His pithy slogans ("A
man's got to know his limitations") were as minatory
as a Magnum; his personal demons kept him as coiled
as a snake. "He's never been afraid of flawed characters," says writer John Lee Hancock, who worked
on Eastwood's *Midnight in the Garden of Good and
Evil*. "That makes him exceptional in this town."

He directs with the same determined unsenti-
mentality, and at 70 has amassed a formidable
body of work, including the moody jazz biopic
Bird and 1992's Oscar winner *Unforgiven*. "He's
not a guy who talks your ear off, but he does listen," says Hancock of his low-key style. Adds old
friend James Garner, who costars in Eastwood's
upcoming *Space Cowboys*, "He's so quiet you never know when the camera's rolling." —B F

27

SIMPLY THE BEST	RAWHIDE (1959–66)	A FISTFUL OF DOLLARS (1964)	DIRTY HARRY (1971)	UNFORGIVEN (1992)	THE BRIDGES OF MADISON COUNTY (1995)
	Rollin', rollin', rollin'... Eastwood charged head-long into the oater genre as cowpoke Rowdy Yates in this CBS series.	Eastwood made a name for himself as the Man With No Name in Sergio Leone's primo spaghetti Western.	Clint must've felt lucky, punk, after he nabbed the maverick-avenger role when Frank Sinatra pulled out.	As director and star, he revisited—and revised—the Western, and rode off with Oscars for Best Director and Best Picture.	He found the genuine sweetness in Robert James Waller's saccharine novel.

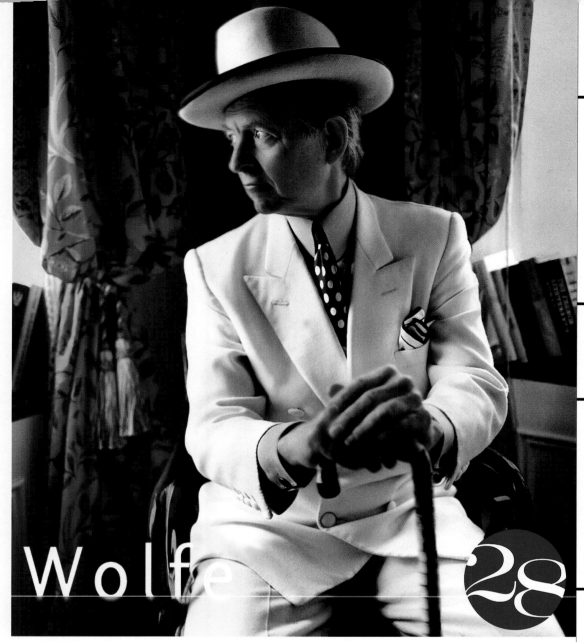

Wolfe 28

PHOTOGRAPH BY MOSHE BRAKHA

YOU WOULDN'T BE HERE IF IT WEREN'T FOR Tom Wolfe. Or, to spin that another way: *We*, as in EW, wouldn't be here. After all, the whole idea that pop culture is something to be chronicled and skewered in all its kaleidoscopic ecstasy and irony—well, that *originated* with him. Just as the Beatles and Bob Dylan were turning rock & roll into a beast to be reckoned with, Wolfe was willing to soil his meringue-white suit on the streets of the vast new Emerald City called Pop. "In the '60s," says Wolfe, 69, "a group of journalists—I wasn't the only one— realized that *the* big story was not the war in Vietnam, but the enormous changes in the way in which people were living."

With that yellow brick road laid out before him, Wolfe set out to make sense of debutantes and astronauts, hippies and yuppies, Cary Grant and Phil Spector. He minted the lingua franca of each era—terms like "radical chic" and "the right stuff." He burrowed into details most reporters are too lazy to investigate. (Just *try* to forget that equine copulation scene from *A Man in Full*.) He liberated journalism by making it…*yeeeeeoooooowwwsahhhhhh!*…a blast to read. "One thing a writer must do is entertain," he says. "I mean, that's your first obligation to a reader." As his books came out—onomatopoeic, exclamation-point-packed romps like *The Electric Kool-Aid Acid Test*, sprawling neo-Thackeray novels like *The Bonfire of the Vanities*—it gradually became clear: Tom Wolfe was defining each decade.

And *still* wearing that white suit. "I felt like a man from Mars," he says, recalling one sojourn in psychedelic San Francisco. "I never took off my suit and tie, so I stuck out. But I've long since learned there's no use trying to blend in." The Wizard of Oz probably felt the same way. —JG

SIMPLY THE BEST

THE KANDY-KOLORED TANGERINE-FLAKE STREAMLINE BABY (1965) Birth of the cool: After years as a conventional journalist, Wolfe lets his prose shatter into a supernova of color, sound, and odd punctuation.

THE ELECTRIC KOOL-AID ACID TEST (1968) The ultimate chronicle of hippiedom

RADICAL CHIC & MAU-MAUING THE FLAK CATCHERS (1970) Wolfe shimmies through America's most dangerous minefield: race relations. He comes out unscathed; everybody else is blown to smithereens.

THE RIGHT STUFF (1979) Covering the early days of the American space program, Wolfe presaged Ronald Reagan and *Top Gun* with this high-octane ode to patriotism and testosterone. It was the basis for the 1983 film.

▲ **THE BONFIRE OF THE VANITIES** (1987) The ultimate chronicle of yuppiedom

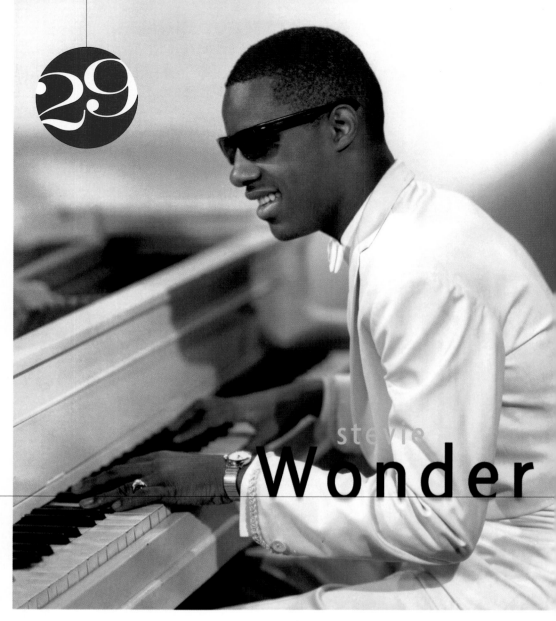

29

Stevie

Wonder

THE 12 YEAR OLD GENIUS (1963)
Not Stevie's finest record, but c'mon, the kid was 12! Hear the harp-blowing prodigy wail like a preteen soul banshee.

MUSIC OF MY MIND (1972)
With "Superwoman" and "Love Having You Around," this was the album where Wonder (now taking on producing, writing, arranging, and virtually all instrumental parts) made the quantum leap from musician to full-fledged artist.

INNERVISIONS (1973)
Wonder's first masterpiece is an R&B juggernaut featuring such hits as "Higher Ground," "Don't You Worry 'Bout a Thing," and the politically explosive "Living for the City."

▲ SONGS IN THE KEY OF LIFE (1976)
His best record—and quite possibly the decade's as well. A double-platter magnum opus ranging from naive pop ("Isn't She Lovely?") to learned rapture ("Sir Duke").

STEVIE WONDER'S ORIGINAL MUSI-QUARIUM I (1982)
From the deep-fried funk of "Superstition" to its giddy conclusion, "Do I Do," this greatest-hits double album belongs in any record collection.

SURE, MOZART MAY HAVE SCRIBBLED HIS FIRST composition when he was 5, but let's be honest: You can't do the Mashed Potato to it. For that alone, when it comes to musical prodigies, we've got to give the edge to Stevie Wonder.

He cut his debut, 1962's *The Jazz Soul of Little Stevie*, at age 11. From the outset, not only was Motown chief Berry Gordy's blind boy wonder a mind-boggling musician, proficient on piano, organ, harmonica, and drums, he could also sing. Perhaps sing is the wrong word: Stevie could *wail*. With the release of his third album, *The 12 Year Old Genius*, the kid with the ear-to-ear smile, swaying like a possessed Pentecostalist channeling the Holy Ghost, had become a soul sensation.

That would be accomplishment enough for most artists, but Wonder was just warming up. Beginning with 1972's *Music of My Mind*, he began producing a staggering canon that would push R&B to lusher, more conceptual heights. Not to say the hit singles dried up: As the complexity of his music deepened, and as his lyrics turned to issues of race and poverty, his popularity only grew. Between 1972 and 1980, Wonder racked up 10 top 10 tunes, including "Superstition" and "You Are the Sunshine of My Life" (*Talking Book*); "Living for the City" and "Higher Ground" (*Innervisions*); and "I Wish" and "Sir Duke" (from his 1976 double-album masterpiece, *Songs in the Key of Life*).

"I remember looking at the album cover of *Songs in the Key of Life* and being kind of frightened...but I felt the power," says D'Angelo, one of countless R&B musicians indebted to Stevie Wonder. "When I was 6 or 7, [my mother] would make me go to the piano and play 'Master Blaster (Jammin')' whenever she had company.... I don't look at Stevie as a human being. He's almost like a deity." Take that, Mozart. —CHRIS NASHAWATY

martin Scorsese

MARTIN SCORSESE WAS A STUDENT OF THE CLASSIC Westerns of John Ford, and in a sense what he has given us is the urban equivalent. The dusty and hardscrabble frontier has been exchanged for the garbage-strewn streets of New York, the larger-than-life heroism of a John Wayne for a motley crew of antiheroes, most often embodied by Scorsese's on-screen doppelgänger Robert De Niro. But the blood-soaked battles of *Taxi Driver*'s Travis Bickle, *Raging Bull*'s Jake La Motta, and *GoodFellas*' Henry Hill are also waged for the American Dream, albeit a warped, sociopathic version of it. And in their single-minded pursuits, they are as egomaniacal as any Ford cavalry soldier—if also fatally insecure, as befits their disenfranchised time. Scorsese's films are "interested in stretching the empathetic powers of the audience and redeeming the unredeemable," notes Peter Biskind, author of *Easy Riders, Raging Bulls: How the Sex-Drugs-and-Rock 'N' Roll Generation Saved Hollywood.*

"It's an attempt to discover a humanity in the worst sort of people—gangsters, depraved prize-fighters, people you'd never invite for dinner…. His moral judgment was a catholic—with a small *c*—acceptance of these characters."

While navigating that bleak universe, Scorsese has virtually come to own the word *gritty* within the film-crit set. But he's also our consummate stylist. Among the first generation of academically schooled filmmakers, he's worn his beloved influences—including Godard, noir, Hitchcock, Hollywood musicals—on his sleeve and in the process given us a crash course in cinema history. More resonantly, he also presaged the future. "In his amalgamation of cinema vérité documentary and a kind of feverish impressionism, he pioneered a new street cinema," says Biskind. "He worked on his own terms and made the kind of films he wanted to make, come hell or high water. He fathered the independent film we have today." —MF

30

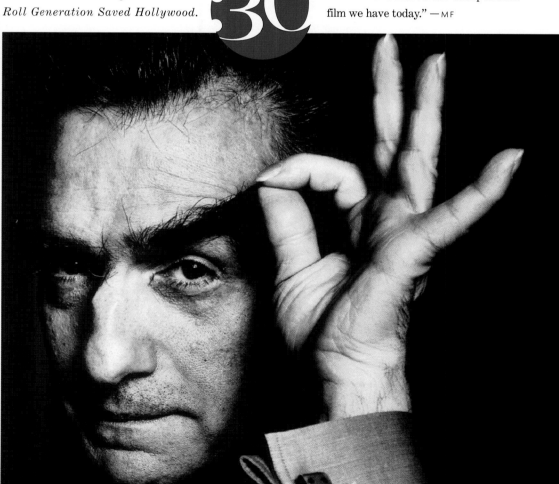

PHOTOGRAPH BY NIGEL PARRY

▲ *THE COLOR PURPLE* (1985)
As Sofia, a young black woman punished for her pride and her passion, Winfrey proved she had more than enough chops to fill the big screen.

THE OPRAH WINFREY SHOW (NATIONAL DEBUT 1986)
Her high-rated chat-fest was first to jump off the "sensationalist" bandwagon and turn the power of talk on to spirituality and female empowerment.

OPRAH'S BOOK CLUB (1996)
The talk-show queen conquered the publishing world when her on-air book club debuted with *The Deep End of the Ocean*. Ever since, any Oprah book club pick is bound for best-seller lists.

BELOVED (1998)
Not a box office hit, but a testament to Winfrey's industry power. She produced and starred in this adaptation of Toni Morrison's tale about a former slave haunted by the ghost of her child.

O (2000)
Winfrey completes her role as the queen of all media with her own monthly magazine.

oprah Winfrey

THANK GOD FOR MISTAKES. "EARLY ON, I WAS IN Barbara Walters mode," Oprah Winfrey says of her eponymous talk show. "Then one day, I mispronounced some words on air and cracked myself up. I realized, 'Gosh, Oprah, you *can* have a natural moment, you *can* do your own thing.'"

Rarely has so much emerged from so little: seismic pop-culture shifts, America's best girlfriend, a media empire!—all because of a fleeting few seconds early in her career. Daytime talk was pioneered by Phil Donahue, but the 46-year-old Winfrey feminized it, colorized it, personalized it (most memorably with a little red wagon filled with 67 pounds of animal fat—symbolizing her weight loss). "I basically make a lot of money being myself," she says. "I sit and talk about what I'm interested in, so the show's evolvement has come from my personal evolvement. Doing it honestly feels like breathing to me. It's the most natural thing I do all day."

And when she catches her breath, she's acting (*The Color Purple*), producing (*Beloved*, which she starred in, and ABC's *Oprah Winfrey Presents*), and helping create best-selling novels (her show's book club has showcased 33 to date). Most recently, she helped launch a cable network for women (Oxygen) and a magazine. Think about it: Nearly 30 years ago, when Winfrey was a TV reporter in Nashville, the idea of a black woman transforming herself into one of the most powerful people in entertainment was beyond implausible. That we take her ascension for granted now is a testament to...well, Oprah just being Oprah.

"People of all backgrounds identify with her because she's never shied away from showing herself, warts and all," says Jeffrey Jacobs, president of her Harpo Entertainment Group. "They know she's made mistakes and she will make mistakes, just like everybody else." Like everybody else? Hardly. —SHAWNA MALCOM

31

paul
Newman

YOU CAN TRY, BUT YOU CAN'T AVOID THEM. SEAR-ing, surreal, almost alien blue—deeply set in a face cribbed from Michelangelo's David. Even at 75, Paul Newman's eyes have a roguish glint, seducing women, men, anything with a pulse.

But, like Newman himself, you can get beyond them. A Cleveland native who abandoned sporting-goods sales to act, Newman has always been a helluva lot more than a gorgeous mug. Not to his mind, of course: "Paul thinks of himself as not having a great deal of natural talent," says Sydney Pollack, who directed Newman in 1981's *Absence of Malice*, "but as someone who has had to work very hard to be as good as he is." The effort (though we hardly noticed) paid off in his characters: Simply put, they are losers. And cads. And hucksters. Guys infused with the very essence of American bravado and grift, and all made lovable, riveting—even mythic—by Newman: "Fast Eddie" Felson, Harper, Cool Hand Luke, Butch Cassidy. "Paul has excellent judgment in choosing parts," says longtime friend and fellow amateur car racer James Garner. "And if you want to stick around, that's something you have to have."

Whether seething with randy hubris in *Hud*, repairing with his angelic shadow, Robert Redford, in *The Sting*, or reprising Fast Eddie as a broken shell in '86's *The Color of Money* (for which he won an Oscar), Newman has been an ever-evolving barometer of cool. Not the nihilistic Dean variety; crafty, laid-back, *survivor* cool. What's more, when you consider he's half of the First Couple of American Cinema (Newman directed wife Joanne Woodward to an Academy Award nomination in '68's *Rachel, Rachel*), it's easy to understand why his glow—like those eyes—has never dimmed. —D F

SIMPLY THE BEST

CAT ON A HOT TIN ROOF (1958)
Newman and Elizabeth Taylor are crystallized at the height of their acting powers in this classic.

THE HUSTLER (1961)
Drenched in alcohol and pool-hall smoke, Newman's turn as "Fast Eddie" Felson is widely considered his best.

COOL HAND LUKE (1967)
As a feisty prisoner on a Southern chain gang, he suffered no failure to communicate.

BUTCH CASSIDY AND THE SUNDANCE KID (1969)
Newman and Redford gun-slinging, sparring, and going down in a hail of bullets

THE VERDICT (1982)
The actor received an Oscar nomination for his role as an alcoholic lawyer who salvages his career and his self-respect.

Star Trek

IS IT POSSIBLE THAT GENE RODDENBERRY IS our generation's Homer?

Before all you classics majors get your togas in a twist, think about it: What is *Star Trek*'s "five-year mission to explore strange new worlds, to seek out new life and new civilizations, to boldly go where no man has gone before" if not a riff on the *Odyssey* at warp speed? "*Star Trek* is our modern mythology," says Roger Nygard, director of the documentary *Trekkies*. "Every episode has travel, adventure, monsters, action, explosions, and romance all wrapped into a moralistic story—which is what mythology is at its best."

If that's the case—and hell, if you've ever picked up a plastic tricorder at a *Trek* convention, then you're already with us on this one—then William Shatner's chick magnet Capt. James T. Kirk must be our swashbuckling Odysseus. Says Roddenberry's successor, *Trek* producer Rick Berman, "Kirk was

the quintessential '60s TV hero, a man who had a babe with a beehive hairdo in one hand and a phaser in the other." Now, just substitute a spear and Greek temptress Circe and, by Jove, we've got a match. As for Leonard Nimoy's Spock, well, that's where *Trek* gets the edge: While the ancients had their logic-minded philosophers, the subtly alien charms of a Vulcan's pointy ears are pure Roddenberry.

Still, even he never anticipated that the show he pitched to TV execs as a "*Wagon Train* to the stars" would live so long and prosper so lucratively. After spinning off three more series, nine feature films, countless imitators, and a race of rabid acolytes (who actually prefer the moniker Trekkers, thank you), it remains the undisputed TV-franchise king. "You could swallow up all the Grateful Dead fans, Madonna fans, and James Bond fans with the sheer number of *Trek* fans," says Nygard. "It's almost like a religion." Almost? —CN

33

IN THE '60S, RICHARD PRYOR GRABBED COMEDY BY its ear—and proceeded to spray a stream of hair-raising expletives into it. But his stand-up was radical not just for its shock value, but because Pryor's comedy was an amped-up take on the neuroses of Richard Pryor—being black chief among them. Hence the title of his 1974 groundbreaking album, *That Nigger's Crazy*.

Mainstream (white) America came to love him best as Gene Wilder's jive buddy in *Silver Streak* and *Stir Crazy*. But as an actor, he was more arresting playing characters like those in his stand-up: the tragic junkie of *Lady Sings the Blues* or the auto assembly worker in Paul Schrader's *Blue Collar*. But his unfulfilled wish was to play jazz great Charlie Parker, and in that role he might have found the closest approximation to his comedy's richly imagined riffs. Like Parker's, Pryor's art was improvisational—fast, wild, and intensely introspective. He spun painful and painfully hilarious stories about characters whose side of the story many hadn't heard before—ones in which winos and pimps were subjects of sympathy and ridicule. "As kids we used to sneak and listen to his records because they were taboo," recalls rapper-actor Ice Cube. "He had a lot of influence on rap. Listen to N.W.A—just having the balls to get up there and use profanity to make our point. If he could say what he wanted to say, why couldn't we?"

On the small screen, Pryor brought his taboo-piercing wit into the safety of American living rooms with the Lily Tomlin CBS specials—the second of which won him an Emmy. Of course, conventional wisdom suggested that such edgy material would not play in Peoria. But Peoria is, literally, Pryor's hometown.

These days, the ravages of multiple sclerosis have cruelly conspired to accomplish what critics and network censors were unable to—quiet the 59-year-old Pryor. Yet in many quarters, his voice can still be heard. Says Ice Cube, "Without Richard Pryor there is no Eddie Murphy, there is no Chris Rock. All these comedians today would be nowhere without Pryor." — C N

34 richard Pryor

SIMPLY THE BEST

LADY SINGS THE BLUES (1972)
Pryor's smack-addled Piano Man steals the show in this biopic of addict/crooner Billie Holiday.

SILVER STREAK (1976)
Finally, his onstage anarchy translates to the big screen in his first pairing with Gene Wilder.

BLUE COLLAR (1978)
In this gut-wrenching working-class drama, he goes for more than laughs as an anguished have-not driven to crime.

STIR CRAZY (1980)
This spoof of crime and prison movies gave Pryor a second go-around with Wilder. "That's right, we bad."

JO JO DANCER, YOUR LIFE IS CALLING (1986)
His directorial effort is a self-portrait of a man stripping himself bare.

bruce
Springsteen

35

MOST ROCK STARS INSPIRE KIDS TO ROCK. BRUCE SPRING-
steen inspires them to write. When filmmaker Edward
Burns was growing up in the blue-collar burbs of Long
Island, he found his muse not in Bergman but in the cinematic epiphanies of the Boss. "What was frustrating
growing up was that I never went to the movies and saw
anybody like me. I was hungry for that. And the only place you
could get it was on a Springsteen album," remembers Burns, who
went on to name his film *She's the One* after a torrential Springsteen anthem. "I just envisioned my town when I heard those
songs. I wanted to try and do the same thing."

Bruce Springsteen has that effect on people. Whether we're
talking about the wild-eyed romantic of *Born to Run* or the cold-
eyed realist of *Tunnel of Love*, the scuzzy wharf rat of "Rosalita"
or the pop-radio Rabbit Angstrom of "Hungry Heart," the Great
Plains Jeremiah of the *Nebraska* demos or the yowling rock & roll
ringmaster who'd turn a stadium into a house party during the
heady 10-times-platinum days of *Born in the U.S.A.*, Springsteen
doesn't just rock your world. He changes it. His own life is an
odyssey of impossible leaps—lonely misfit from that legendary
New Jersey "town full of losers" becomes a mass-media, 45-
million-selling supernova—and his music is a reflection of that
journey. Tap into it and it transforms you. It made Melissa
Etheridge grab a guitar and head out of Kansas. It made Sean
Penn leap into the fraternal fires of *The Indian Runner*. (Penn's
directorial debut was based on Springsteen's
"Highway Patrolman.")

Through all his mutations, though,
the Boss, now 50, has held on to a core
sense of self. "Springsteen, you always knew, was not gonna die
stupid," Bono said upon inducting him into the Rock and Roll Hall
of Fame in 1999. "He didn't buy the mythology that screwed so
many people. Instead he created an alternative mythology, one
where ordinary lives became extraordinary and heroic." —JG

SIMPLY THE BEST

THE WILD, THE INNOCENT AND THE E STREET SHUFFLE (1973)
Impossibly romantic songs of the big city, young love, and the Jersey boardwalk

BORN TO RUN (1975)
Springsteen's back-against-the-wall breakthrough. A glittering rock & roll rhap-sody. This is where you can hear "She's the One."

DARKNESS ON THE EDGE OF TOWN (1978)
Sweaty, oily, loud, and clenched—like a howl from the assembly line

NEBRASKA (1982)
Americans wanted brain-less, glossy pop—the Boss gave them a bleak, beauti-ful, raw-demo song cycle about poverty and murder.

BORN IN THE U.S.A. (1984)
It may seem as bombastic as a three-ring circus, but desperation haunts songs like "My Hometown."

36

james Brown

SIMPLY THE BEST

WHEN FUNK'S SECOND-GREATEST SHOWMAN (George Clinton) talks about funk's greatest showman (James Brown), he gets a little excited: "S---, he's the bomb. The bomb! Man, he's pure dope! James' funk funks 100 percent at a time; most people funkin' two if they're *lucky*."

James Brown never did anything less than 100 percent. His gospel bark of a voice was as extreme and powerful as any instrument you'll hear; his stage moves were jaw-droppingly gymnastic. But his greatest talents—as a songwriter, arranger, and bandleader—are often forgotten amid the spectacle of his live shows. From his earliest soul-singer days with the Famous Flames (1953–1968) through several incarnations of JB, Brown had an unmatched knack for assembling sharp musicians and teaching them to hear music the way he did.

Which is the definition of funk, really: hearing music the way James Brown does. Just turn on the radio. Every rhythmic grunt, that's James Brown. Every muffled guitar scratch, that's James Brown. Syncopated bass lines, delayed snare hits, staccato horn blasts—James Brown, James Brown, James Brown. If you're listening to hip-hop, you're listening to James Brown, often literally, courtesy of sampling.

You get the point. With polyrhythmic masterpieces like "Papa's Got a Brand New Bag, Pt. 1" Brown invented modern dance music, paving the way for Sly, Prince, Timbaland, and just about any other rhythm-obsessed musician you can think of. "His concept was to be number one, and that meant a lot of preparation," says former JB saxophonist Maceo Parker. "People looked at him to set trends. Everyone tried to copy us, and there was a lot of pride in that." Still, his greatest achievement is his own work. As he writes in *James Brown: The Godfather of Soul* (about disco, but you can apply it to most post-JB sounds): "See, I taught 'em everything they know but not everything I know." —ROB BRUNNER

LIVE AT THE APOLLO (1963)
Pre-funk James at his most inspired, this is the best recorded evidence of the legendary live performances that earned him that "hardest-working man in show business" title.

"PAPA'S GOT A BRAND NEW BAG, PT. 1" (1965)
The birth of funk. With a tricky rhythm and scratchy guitar, Brown creates a syncopated new sound that fundamentally changes R&B.

"COLD SWEAT" (1967)
The funkiest song ever? More than seven minutes long, this stutter-beat groove is polyrhythmic perfection.

"SAY IT LOUD— I'M BLACK AND I'M PROUD" (1968)
Revolutionary politics go mainstream when this rousing Black Power anthem hits No. 10 on the pop charts.

"FUNKY DRUMMER" (1970)
"One, two, three, four, hit it," Brown shouts, and JB's stickman Clyde Stubblefield taps out what would become the world's most familiar drum break.

harrison
Ford

IN ANY POLL, IN ANY YEAR, HARRISON FORD IS THE people's choice—the man you can count on to play a man you can count on. Even when he's cast as a rogue (and few classic characters exhibit more scoundrel potential than *Star Wars*' Han Solo, at least before rehabilitation by Princess Leia and the salubrious effects of the Force), Ford projects the moral heft of archetypal American heroes. And for over 20 years, his archetypes have been good for business: Starring in 3 of the 10 biggest films of all time, he's the movie star Hollywood can rely on, gross for gross, for a box office score.

A Ford man makes a good President (*Air Force One*) or airplane pilot (*Six Days, Seven Nights*) or lawman (*Blade Runner, Witness*). But a Ford man also struggles with inner conflict, and keeps his mouth shut, which makes him a good CIA opera- tive (*Patriot Games, Clear and Present Danger*) or corporate type (*Working Girl*) or guy on the lam (*The Fugitive*).

Of course, a Ford man also looks real good in a fedora or pushing the throttle of the *Millennium Falcon*, which is what has allowed the actor who wanted to be a forest ranger or a coal worker (and who was once voted Sexiest Man Alive by PEOPLE magazine) to play Indiana Jones-size adventurers without looking one whit foolish.

Audiences love Ford because he wears his celebrity like it's just that, a hat or business suit he might throw off and leave on the freeway. An anti-schmoozer who lives part-time in Wyoming, he's as excited about analyzing his success as about dawdling in a pit writhing with snakes. "My plan has always been to do all kinds of films for all kinds of audiences," he says tersely. "I really think about preserving my opportunities. And being useful." His steady utility is his most heroic quality. —LS

"BEFORE ANYONE HAD EVER HEARD OF HER," SAYS director Sydney Pollack, "Jane Fonda told me, 'This girl is great. This girl is a genius.'" Fonda was prepping *The Electric Horseman* with Pollack in '78 when she delivered that prognosis, formulated while watching Streep steal every small scene she had in *Julia*, Streep's '77 film debut. By the time Pollack worked with her on '85's *Out of Africa*, she'd already cut her patrician-looking teeth on lead roles in *The French Lieutenant's Woman* and *Sophie's Choice*. Much is made of her technical command, of her way with a diphthong (she's mastered more dialects than Henry Higgins). But frankly, she wearies of such hosannas. "For me, it's the least interesting part of the discussion about my work," says Streep, 51. Rather, her power lies in her uncanny, unearthly ability to inhabit whomever she plays. Timeless, incandescent beauty helps, but so does grueling manual labor. For her performance as a violin teacher in 1999's *Music of the Heart*, she learned to play the instrument from scratch through four to six hours of daily practice over two months. "There is no way to fake it," she explains. "I didn't know any other way to do it." The practice made perfect, though. In February, the Academy rewarded the actress with her 12th nomination (for Best Actress), allowing Streep to tie Katharine Hepburn's all-time-high tally. Sorry, Katharine. —SD

meryl
Streep

miles
Davis

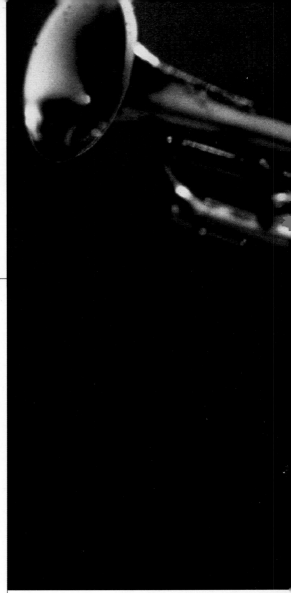

AS A PERFORMER, MILES DAVIS MADE AN OCCA-
sional, if over-publicized, habit of turning his back to
the audience. "Look, man, all I am is a trumpet player," he once explained. "I ain't no entertainer, and
ain't trying to be one. I am one thing, a musician."

Rejection was the one consistent key in Davis'
creative life. Gently but willfully, he turned his
back on each of his musical pasts, creating a
groundbreaking stylistic trope at each rotation.
When, for instance, he'd shaken off the sweaty fre-
neticism of bebop after a stint with the Charlie
Parker Quintet, he made his first splash as a bandleader with 1949's sparely urbane *Birth of the
Cool*. And 20 years later, after he'd stretched jazz
strictures to their outer limits, Davis exploded the
genre with an infusion of rock rhythm and snarling
polytonality, producing the violently unremitting
Bitches Brew. Between these two flash points, in
1959, Davis ditched traditional methods of impro-
visation in favor of floating above and around a series of scales. The hauntingly restrained result,
Kind of Blue, is, as Quincy Jones once suggested,
the proper answer to "What is jazz?"

Davis didn't navigate his uncharted course alone.
"He had a magical gift for knowing how other mu-
sicians fit around his musical ideas," says Ron
Carter, the bassist in his virtuoso '60s quintet. Yet
only as revered—and often vitriolic—a master as
Davis could have compelled a John Coltrane or
John McLaughlin to shun convention. He was the
Prince of Darkness, the Evil Genius, and, ultimate-
ly, our truest musical revolutionary. —WILL LEE

norman Lear

IF TV HAS A EUGENE O'NEILL, IT'S NORMAN LEAR.
"He dealt with real life, and that's what set him
apart," says Martin Mull, star of the producer's
scarily prescient 1977 talk-show parody, *Fernwood
2-Night*. "My generation felt that we were going
after truth and beauty, and we weren't going to

PHOTOGRAPH BY DARRYL ESTRINE

stand for the glitz, the glossed-over. And here comes Norman, a champion of that."

Lear's brand of beauty wasn't the kind you find in fashion magazines; it came from ripping the lid off convention. With an unparalleled string of Nielsen-topping sitcoms in the '70s, he forever gave the lie to TV's whitewashed suburban "normality," offering glimpses into the worlds of upwardly mobile minorities (*The Jeffersons*), "reverse" bigotry (*Sanford and Son*), black blue-collar family life (*Good Times*), and single parenting (*One Day at a Time*).

And then there was Archie Bunker. Lear's most infamous creation—a bigoted, abusive working stiff from Queens, N.Y.—was born on Jan. 12, 1971, on a show called *All in the Family*. It was Lear's particular genius to fashion characters who provoked as they amused, and in that regard Bunker, as played by Carroll O'Connor, was his magnum opus. Irresistible to

both the Joe Sixpacks who lionized him for his "good old days" rants and the liberals who saw in him a dangerous anachronism refuting the hard-won gains of the feminist, civil rights, and antiwar movements, Bunker became—and remains—a symbol for the end of an era. "I never looked at Archie as a hater," says Lear. "He was a fearful man. Things were changing too fast around him. [It was] a fear born of ignorance. And fear can often play as anger."

Lear, says Mull, "brought a certain enlightenment that is now common knowledge." The man himself, now 77, is perhaps the only one who takes his legacy for granted. "I'd be some kind of fool if, after a couple of thousand years of the Judeo-Christian ethic we still haven't erased bigotry and hatred, [and I thought] that my little situation comedy had some effect. But I think it got people to talk." And, more impressive still, to laugh. —MF

40

SIMPLY THE BEST

▲ *ALL IN THE FAMILY* (DEBUTED 1971)
With the inimitable Archie Bunker's help, he transformed an outer-borough living room into an absurdist crucible of national unrest. Political tumult was never so much fun.

SANFORD AND SON (1972–77)
As if to prove that bigotry and bluster transcend race, Lear painted a portrait of part-time junkman and full-time curmudgeon in Redd Foxx's irascible Fred Sanford.

MAUDE (1972–78)
In the first of many *All in the Family* spin-offs, Bea Arthur wrought a brassy embodiment of Archie's worst nightmare: a tough, liberal, intellectually independent (gasp!) woman.

THE JEFFERSONS (1975–85)
Prime-time TV itself was elevated with George and Weezy's move on up to the East Side, as Lear gave us a hysterical glimpse into the world of middle-class black America.

MARY HARTMAN, MARY HARTMAN (1976–77)
As breathtakingly bizarre now as the day it premiered, Stormin' Norman's surreal dramedy lifted the veil on small-town domesticity long before *Twin Peaks*.

41 james **Dean**

LIVED FAST. DIED YOUNG. LEFT A GOOD-LOOKING CORPSE. THE cliché was invented for James Dean. Three movies: *Rebel Without a Cause, Giant, East of Eden.* Then a 1955 car crash that mangled his Porsche 550 Spyder on a deserted road in Paso Robles, Calif. Dean, just shy of 25, was nearly decapitated. Maybe the cliché is wrong. The corpse wasn't so good-looking after all. Still, how cool. And needless. And stupid.

Who would he have become? The historical record suggests, at best, that he might have become the Marlon Brando we really wanted—a Brando who never got fat or weird or made bad choices. He and Brando came up the same way, through brilliant early work in New York theater that ended up buying them tickets to Hollywood. They both played rebels. They both worked with Elia Kazan. They both roiled with a kind of sexuality the movies hadn't seen before—Brando's dangerous and animal, Dean's tender, vulnerable, nearly feminine.

The truth is, Dean could have become a lesser light, a Steve McQueen. He could have made more of the foolish, impetuous choices that he was already making when he got into his Porsche. He was a young man obsessed with death in the romantic-tragic-brooding-loner way that a million young men have since tried to imitate. Says fellow actor Rod Steiger, "He gave me his prized copy of *Death in the Afternoon* by Hemingway. Every line that dealt with death was underlined in red pencil. I saw that and said, 'Oh boy.'" So even if he had survived the '50s, who's to say he would have survived the '60s?

"I don't want to achieve immortality through my work," Woody Allen once said. "I want to achieve it through not dying." Dean did the opposite. His death turned him from a promising and talented young actor into a symbol, a refrigerator magnet, a glossy postcard, a male Marilyn who never even had the chance to make the mistakes she made. A ghost of unfulfilled promise, Dean stands for all of our Hollywood dreams of what could have been. —MARK HARRIS

SIMPLY THE BEST

EAST OF EDEN (1955)
The film that made James Dean a star, *Eden* (based on the John Steinbeck novel) was a showcase for the unsettling angst that bubbled just beneath the young star's surface.

REBEL WITHOUT A CAUSE (1955)
The red jacket. The T-shirt. The brooding glances. In *Rebel*, released shortly after his fatal car accident, Dean's performance became a touchstone for sullen teens the world over, even to this day.

GIANT (1956)
Dean was nominated posthumously for an Oscar for his pathos-filled performance as Jett Rink, a Texas rancher who strikes it rich with oil. The performance would help seal Dean's status as a legend for decades.

francis ford
Coppola

"I BELIEVE IN AMERICA…"

The famous opening scene of his 1972 masterpiece, *The Godfather*, tells us a lot about its director: Francis Ford Coppola is optimistic enough to buy into the idea of the American Dream, but also realistic enough to know that its nightmare flip side usually prevails. By the end of the Oscar-winning crime-family saga, the Corleones have attained that dream—but they've also sold their souls to get it. It's what makes the film and its 1974 sequel the closest thing we have to a national mythology.

Strangely enough, Coppola bristles at being synonymous with his Italian-American epic: "I'm not interested in *The Godfather*," he told ENTERTAINMENT WEEKLY in '97, "but I recognize that we hit something in the culture. To my shock it was successful, but it kind of suckered me into a career different than I planned."

And that should tell you another thing about Coppola: In his disregard for mainstream success, he stands in for every artist who has overreached. His missteps are inseparable from his masterpieces. Soaring ambition sometimes produces *The Godfather*, and sometimes *One From the Heart*. Be grateful for both—even Coppola's failures fall to earth like spectacular comets, as his successes rocket into the history books.

Still, the director always thought that his legacy would be as the David who stood up to the studio Goliaths. Sure, he's thrived inside the system (his movies have racked up 54 Oscar nominations; he himself has won five). But like the underdog heroes of *The Conversation*, *Tucker: The Man and His Dream*, *John Grisham's The Rainmaker*, even *Apocalypse Now*, he yearns to be a maverick—the guy who *didn't* sell his soul to achieve his dream.

"That's the Holy Grail, whether you're Martin Scorsese or some 24-year-old kid borrowing money from your uncle," Coppola said. "You want to make personal films." It's just our luck that this storyteller's personal vision is also universal. —CN

42

tom
Hanks

**SIMPLY
THE BEST**

BIG (1988)
By getting in touch with his inner child, Hanks charmed the world and landed the title of America's favorite actor.

PHILADELPHIA (1993)
His poignant portrayal of a gay lawyer with AIDS secured Hanks' standing as a serious dramatic actor and won him his first Oscar.

SLEEPLESS IN SEATTLE (1993)
With charm, humor, and a touch of deep sadness, he proved that even nice guys can be romantic leads.

FORREST GUMP (1994)
Playing an Everyman with a double-digit IQ may have been his smartest move; he earned an Oscar and, some say, more than $50 million.

SAVING PRIVATE RYAN (1998)
Hanks turned what might have been an anonymous soldier role into the heart and soul of the front line.

FORGET EVERY TIRED DESCRIPTION you've read. Forget "nice." Forget "regular guy." Forget "average joe." Like his cinematic forebear Jimmy Stewart, Tom Hanks, 44, has been sorely underestimated for far too long. Yes, he's friendly and polite; almost everybody who's ever met him testifies that he treats people with respect. But...nice? The word implies "pushover," it flirts with "Milquetoast," and those words simply do not apply to a man who clawed his way back from dreck like the 1987 film *Dragnet* to become the most commercially bankable star of the '90s. "Nice" doesn't really describe a mainstream actor who had the guts to play a gay man with AIDS—considered career suicide up until his Oscar-winning turn in *Philadelphia*.

Let's blow "average" to bits, too. "Average" means "Matthew Perry movie." Hanks has spearheaded the most critically acclaimed box office phenomena of our age—*Forrest Gump* and *Big*,

43

Apollo 13 and *Saving Private Ryan*. He does what movie stars are supposed to do: He gets a green light for smart flicks that would otherwise wither in development hell. Nothing "regular" about that—or his painstaking film preparation: For *Apollo 13*, he gobbled up microscopic factoids about space travel; for *Ryan*, he turned into a walking World War II encyclopedia.

So let's try some new words in our exegesis of Hanks: "passionate," "bold," and—if you *must*— "decent." Consider a story told by actor Doug Hutchison, who worked with Hanks on 1999's *The Green Mile*. "On his lunch break one day," Hutchison says, "Tom put his hands and footprints into cement at Mann's Chinese Theatre. He came back to the set with cement still on his soles, simply to read lines off camera with me. Anyone could have read with me, but Tom honored his commitment. You can't fake that kind of integrity." —DH

bob
Marley

IF YOU'RE EVEN VAGUELY FAMILIAR WITH THE term *reggae*, you're certainly aware that Bob Marley was its greatest singer. But that's like describing Michael Jordan as merely the best Chicago Bull.

Forget about reggae. Marley was as soulful a singer as Al Green or Sam Cooke, wrapping his patois-sweetened croon around stirring ballads like "Stir It Up." He was as vocal and passionate an advocate for the underclass as Bob Dylan or the Clash in such protest classics as "Get Up, Stand Up." And he was as important a global pop star as anybody of his era, with his greatest-hits collection, 1984's *Legend*, selling more than 10 million copies in the U.S. alone (it still frequently tops *Billboard*'s catalog charts). Other than John Lennon, it's hard to think of another musician who so successfully translated activism and artistic integrity into massive mainstream success. "I actually think he's had more impact and influence than anybody," says Island Records founder Chris Blackwell, who signed the Wailers (Marley and vocalists Peter Tosh and Bunny Livingstone) to Island in 1972. "In any corner of the world you go to, his music is there."

44

If Marley's fame had one drawback, it was in overshadowing Jamaica's other great musicians. Still, it's hard not to be awed by his musical impact (the Fugees are among the most recent acts to cover a Marley tune) or his spiritual presence, still thriving almost 20 years after his death from cancer. "Bob Marley is one of the people that was ordained by the Almighty to get his message to the world," says his justifiably biased son Stephen, who produced *Chant Down Babylon*, a star-studded tribute album released in 1999. "He from the country, then he leave from the country to the ghetto, then he leave from the ghetto to the whole world, all from this little island of Jamaica. He was ordained, anointed, a messenger." —RB

45

NO MATTER WHERE YOU HAPPENED TO BE ON ANY given weeknight between 1962 and 1992—your own bedroom, the bar around the corner—chances are by 11:30 you'd be cozying up to Johnny Carson. At its peak, about 4 out of every 10 homes tuned in to NBC's *The Tonight Show*. There was simply no place like it: Doc on the trumpet, Ed on the couch, and Johnny behind his desk—a sleek visual syntax equaling emotional shelter.

His timing (so sharp Carson would become the measuring shtick for all future late-night hosts), his charming bent for double entendres—they are justifiably legendary. But Carson's faculty extends far beyond the ability to amuse. A Hollywood fixture as entrenched as Schwab's drugstore, Carson had an uncanny ability to switch, in the space of a commercial break, from provocative stand-up comic to facile celeb schmoozer to the paternal host who at heart remained the Nebraska son of a local utility manager. "He was a great baseball catcher," says his pal Don Rickles, who continues to see the firmly retired Carson, now 74. "You could throw shots at him and he always came back making you look good. He had this outstanding comfort zone that made guests feel they were the best person in the room."

The zone extended to his vast audience, all of whom felt like they were in that room. Carson didn't merely entertain, he presided over a national town hall. More than any politician, says *Tonight* exec producer Peter Lassally, "he had this enormous power in that, whatever he was saying or feeling, he was the one voice that everybody felt comfortable with." Eight years after his May 22, 1992, farewell show, we're still waiting for one voice to unite us again. — DS

johnny Carson

james l. Brooks

TO FULLY APPRECIATE JAMES L. BROOKS, CONSIDER THE FLOP. *I'll Do Anything*, the writer-director-producer's ambitious 1994 comedy, contains perhaps the keenest put-down of the lowbrow '90s: "Don't you have to know something besides how to pose for this picture of you that nobody is snapping?"

Our point? Even when Brooks is failing, he's delivering crackling morsels unseen since the brainier heyday of Billy Wilder. And when he's succeeding, you get feasts—sharp-witted confections balanced, feather-light, between heartbreak and hilarity: *Terms of Endearment*, *Broadcast News*, *As Good as It Gets*.

Oscar-nominated films are the least of it, though. The former CBS newswriter and NYU dropout claims a remarkable 15 Emmys for such decade-defining sitcoms as *The Mary Tyler Moore Show* and *The Simpsons*. "Every second I was in his company, I had to try to ignore the knowledge that I was in the presence of genius," says Moore.

Certainly he is the sort of director who can delineate an entire personality with a single neurotic twitch. "I had a mentor who insisted you do research until you screamed," says Brooks, 60, who interviewed a slew of cabbies before creating *Taxi*. And once he's prepared, he displays another uncommon sensibility: Brooks always overestimates the intelligence of his audience. "At a certain point, I don't have a reverse gear," he says. "I can't throw things out." Fortunately, he's passing that legacy on to another generation of comic auteurs, including Wes Anderson and Owen Wilson (*Rushmore*). "There's no one out there like him," says Anderson, who, along with Wilson, was enlisted by Brooks to join an intensive one-on-two workshop while writing *Rushmore*. "You can say to him, 'Here's the situation, what's the funny line?' He'll not only come up with something funny, but something truly bizarre. He has the most original mind of anyone I know." — JS

SIMPLY THE BEST

CARNAC THE MAGNIFICENT
The answer: This punchline-prone psychic. The question: Who is one of Carson's most enduring characters?

THE WEDDING (1969)
Tiny Tim and Miss Vicki tie the knot on stage. A goofy gag done in good taste. Could anyone besides Carson pull this off?

THE FINAL *TONIGHT* SHOW (1992)
Carson takes a quiet, teary, introspective moment on stage to bid adieu. A class act to the end.

SIMPLY THE BEST

TAXI (1978–83)
As a creator and writer of this Emmy-award-winning TV show, Brooks found humor, poignancy, and drama in a bunch of New York cabbies.

jackie
Gleason

47

BURSTING ONTO OUR FLICKERING SCREENS IN A WHIRLWIND OF Falstaffian bluster and Irish blarney, Jackie Gleason was, for a time, America itself. Offstage, he was the epitome of the hard-drinking, chain-smoking "pal" of '50s saloon life. In his work, though, Gleason never forgot his Brooklyn tenement roots, imbuing each of his comic alter egos (from bon vivant Reginald Van Gleason 3d to Joe the Bartender) with a pointed class consciousness—and none more so than his greatest creation, bus driver Ralph Kramden.

In one breathless run of 39 "classic" episodes (1955–56), *The Honeymooners* (costarring Audrey Meadows, Art Carney, and Joyce Randolph) gave the masses their truest reflection: pie-in-the-sky schemer Ralph was our reckless excesses and eternal optimism writ larger than life; his long-suffering wife, Alice, our steady, salt-of-the-earth core. That neither could live without the other put them—and us—over the moon.

By all accounts, Gleason's outsize frame was matched by his ego. Norman Lear, who wrote gags for the young Gleason, makes a much-echoed appraisal: "He was brilliant to the point of genius—brilliant and difficult." Sadly, Gleason's mercurial willfulness kept him from getting dramatic parts; his masterful, Oscar-nominated performance as aging pool shark Minnesota Fats in 1961's *The Hustler* offers a glimpse of what might have been. No less a figure than Laurence Olivier lauded him as one of the finest actors he'd ever worked with after they had costarred in a TV movie (1983's *Mr. Halpern and Mr. Johnson*). In a snub worthy of the luckless Kramden, Gleason (who died of cancer in '87) was never honored with an Emmy for his *Honeymooners* work. His biographer James Bacon speaks for us all when he says, "It's something the academy will never live down." —MF

SIMPLY THE BEST

TERMS OF ENDEARMENT (1983)
His tenure as a triple threat—writer-director-producer—began with this Best Picture winner.

BROADCAST NEWS (1987)
Brooks wore three hats again on this first-rate dramedy about a love triangle at a D.C. news program.

THE JACKIE GLEASON SHOW (DEBUTS 1952)
This variety show is where The Great One earned his moniker, mostly due to a running sketch called...

THE HONEYMOONERS (1955–56)
In 39 unforgettable half hours, he presided over the single most resonant sitcom season in television history.

THE HUSTLER (1961)
Switching gears again, Gleason went dramatic as Minnesota Fats, a role sublimely suited to his larger-than-life visage.

jane Fonda

48

EXCEPT PERHAPS MADONNA, THERE'S NO MORE FERVENT HIGH priestess of reinvention—professional, political, physical—than Jane Fonda. Metamorphosing from sex kitten to serious actress, from "Hanoi Jane" to semiconservative Mrs. Ted Turner, from bulimic to driven fitness guru, Fonda, now 62, has never stopped transforming.

She grew up in a powerful vacuum. Her mother, Frances, killed herself when Jane was 12. Her father, Henry, a model citizen in movies, was a sour, remote disciplinarian. As Jane developed what one producer called "El Greco shanks," she attended Vassar, studied art in Paris, and modeled. Then, in 1958, she faced her fear of working in Dad's shadow and enrolled in the Actors Studio (Lee Strasberg said he admitted her because "there was such panic in her eyes"). She made stage and screen debuts at 22 and spent the next decade decorating frothy comedies (*Tall Story, Barefoot in the Park*) and sexploitative fare masterminded by first husband Roger Vadim (climaxing, literally, in 1968's *Barbarella*).

All that changed with *They Shoot Horses, Don't They?* The 1969 allegory about dance marathoners "was her first serious movie, and she did enormous research," recalls director Sydney Pollack. "She and Red Buttons and I stayed up dancing all night, to see what that level of fatigue was like. Did you get tired in the arms first? The feet? She had to know." Over the next 23 years, Fonda inhabited one raised-consciousness character after another, from a hooker in *Klute* (her first Oscar) to a Vietnam vet's wife in *Coming Home* (her second) to a newscaster in *The China Syndrome*. She picked the unsympathetic roles Bette Davis might have; she didn't fear brittle or hard.

In 1992, Fonda retired. Now she's known mainly as a motivator in workout togs. But she never went for the burn more inspirationally than as an actress. Watch her in anything and behold how she makes performance the ultimate self-improvement. —SD

49

julia Roberts

JULIA ROBERTS TURNED DOWN *SLEEPLESS IN SEATTLE*. SHE refused *Shakespeare in Love*. She worried that people would tire of her continually playing the lovelorn ingenue. What she didn't realize is what moviegoers have always known: We want—no, we need—Julia Roberts to be in love.

Not since Audrey Hepburn has there been a star as winning at playing up both the funny and bittersweet sides of romance. As an actress, Roberts has the range for dark-hued dramas: Witness her drawing upon pools of raw emotion as Sally Field's sickly daughter in *Steel Magnolias*, or clenching in paranoid intensity as a fugitive law student in *The Pelican Brief*. But in her romantic comedies, from *Pretty Woman* to *My Best Friend's Wedding* to *Notting Hill*, she becomes artless. Her passion and belief transform us: She flashes her supernova of a smile, and we are giddy; she yearns, and our hearts break, again and again.

Of course, the paradox of Roberts is that she affects us on this base level while maintaining the soaring glamour of Hollywood royalty. "She has that mysterious element that makes stars stars," says her *Runaway Bride* costar Hector Elizondo. And there's no bigger female star on the planet: As the hands-down box office queen of the '90s (her films regularly break the $100 million barrier), she became the highest-paid actress in Hollywood history, garnering $20 million for *Erin Brockovich*. That heady status, combined with a hectic romantic life, keeps her a gossip-column staple. Julia leaves Kiefer Sutherland at the altar! Julia marries Lyle Lovett in a shocker!

Such offscreen baggage can be deadly to an actor, especially one whose success is dependent upon her ability to draw on our sympathies. But it only adds to Roberts' allure. "Her magic," says former Fox exec Joe Roth, who cast her in *Sleeping With the Enemy*, "is that she convinces us she's a movie queen and the girl next door." In other words, the woman we can't wait to fall in love with, once more. —BC

SIMPLY THE BEST

BAREFOOT IN THE PARK (1967)
Fonda couldn't have had more charm—or delivered the sitcom-ish dialogue with more natural panache.

THEY SHOOT HORSES, DON'T THEY? (1969)
She dives into the alienated depths of a Depression-era marathon dancer.

KLUTE (1971)
Fonda's best role. The languorous bangs of her shag couldn't hide the fear and loneliness in stalked call girl Bree Daniel's eyes.

COMING HOME (1978)
She's too magnificent to believe as a wallflower, but her heart's in the right place.

THE CHINA SYNDROME (1979)
Fonda's feverish earnestness on social issues is part of what makes her so appealing.

PRETTY WOMAN (1990)

The depiction of a prostitute's life may be seriously rosy, but Roberts was just as seriously a star.

▲ MY BEST FRIEND'S WEDDING (1997)

After thrashing about in bad movies for a few years, she hopped back on track in this feisty comedy.

NOTTING HILL (1999)

Playing a movie star—what a stretch. Yet Roberts is both believable and radiantly touching.

RUNAWAY BRIDE (1999)

Back with Richard Gere in the kind of gentle screwball comedy they supposedly don't make anymore

▲ ERIN BROCK-OVICH (2000)

Roberts roared into the new century with sass, killer heels—and a hit drama.

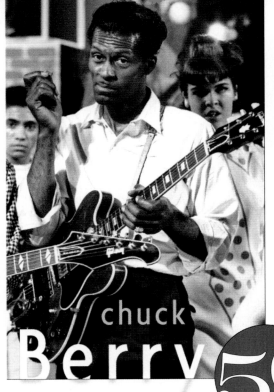

chuck Berry **50**

THERE'S A SCENE IN TAYLOR HACKFORD's 1987 Chuck Berry documentary/concert film *Hail! Hail! Rock 'n' Roll* in which Jerry Lee Lewis recalls arguing with Berry over which of them is "the King of rock & roll." As Lewis recounts, Berry settled the dispute with his fists, effectively whupping his rival. The anecdote is telling—like many great artists, Berry is mercurial. "Chuck can be a pip," says Keith Richards (who once found himself on the business end of a Berry haymaker). "But at moments, he's one of the most charming people you could meet. It's a mood-swing thing."

Or at least a left-hook thing. Still, how many lovers of rock & roll might be moved to violence by the mere suggestion that Berry is anything less than the King? Yeah, yeah, we know—50 million Elvis fans have different ideas. But remember: Elvis was a performer, not a songwriter. Berry was a full-fledged auteur, the guy responsible not only for the riffs that remain the cornerstone of rock guitar, but for two or three dozen of the music's pithiest and most enduring songs, including "Johnny B. Goode," "Back in the USA," and "School Days."

A natural storyteller, Berry sang about typical teenage concerns (cars, dancing, romance) while somehow managing to infuse his lyrics with wry social commentary and sharply etched populist poetry. His joyous, galvanic sound served notice that a new day was dawning and provided a rallying cry for an emerging generation of beat-happy kids. *Roll over, Beethoven/Tell Tchaikovsky the news.* Has anyone said it better?

Most mortals would retire on such cred, but at 73, Berry is still duck-walkin' his way through electric live gigs. As John Lennon once quipped, "If you tried to give rock & roll another name, you might call it 'Chuck Berry.'" —TS

BEFORE SOME CALLED HIM THE GREATEST Guitarist of All Time, James Marshall Hendrix was a scuffling musician eking out a hardscrabble living on the so-called chitlin circuit in the early '60s. In 1964, he accepted a cushy gig playing for the Isley Brothers, a deal that allowed him to live rent-free at the group's Teaneck, N.J., home. Ernie Isley, who was 12 at the time, recalls that Hendrix carried his guitar everywhere—even to the breakfast table. "You would ask him, 'Do you want some orange juice?' and he would sing 'Yee-aaa-hhh' while hitting a note on his guitar—and the note would match the pitch of his voice perfectly."

Hendrix's kinship with his instrument would pay off handsomely. By the time the Seattle-born rocker unveiled the Jimi Hendrix Experience at 1967's Monterey Pop Festival, it was clear his sideman days were over. His nearly erotic stage act involved humping his guitar, playing it with his **51** teeth, even burning it, all the while releasing mind-bending oceans of sound through the artful use of distortion, feedback, and wah-wah. "Music, sweet music—I wish I could caress, caress, caress," he sang on his first album, *Are You Experienced?*, and, indeed, it sometimes seemed Hendrix was literally married to his guitar. It would take his drug-related death, on Sept. 18, 1970, at age 27, to separate them.

Three decades later, the influence—and music—of Hendrix is ubiquitous: it lives on in the pop charts (where his posthumous albums continue to land), in the frankly sexual stylings of Prince, and in the more pedantic world of advertising. And somewhere, right now, a fledgling ax slinger is struggling to figure out just how the master harnessed that astonishing vortex of sound. It's a noble effort but probably a vain one: Whatever his secrets, Jimi Hendrix took them with him. —TS

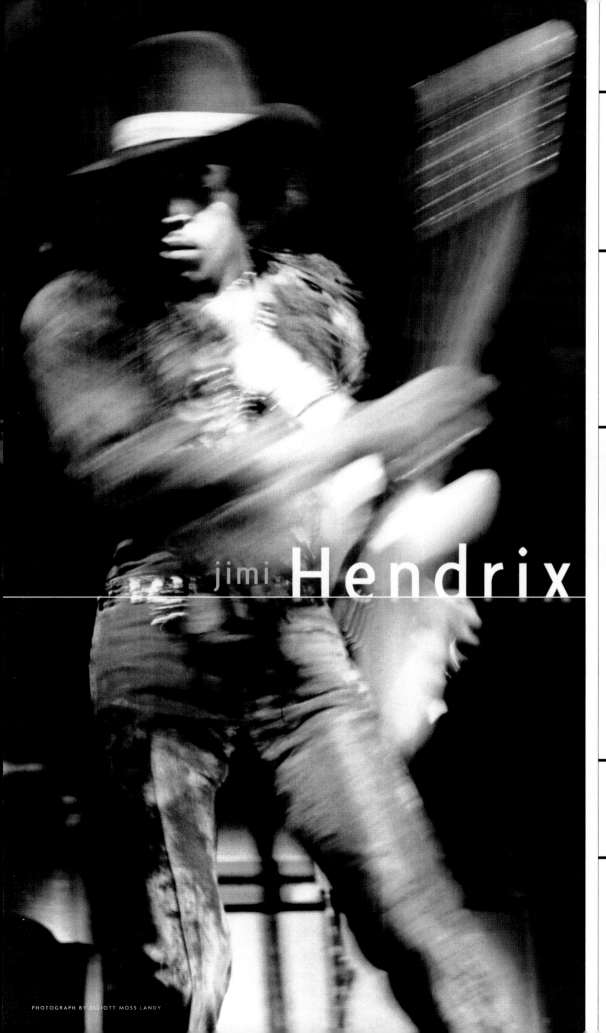

jimi **Hendrix**

SIMPLY THE BEST

ARE YOU EXPERIENCED? (1967)

From the bracing chords that announce "Purple Haze" to the title track's brain-bending backward guitar solo, Hendrix's debut is still mind-blowing after all these years.

ELECTRIC LADYLAND (1968)

Among the delights on this sprawling double-disc opus: a 19-minute aural portrait of life under the sea, a voodoo child's cry of love, and the most intensely lyrical Dylan cover ever

▲ "THE STAR-SPANGLED BANNER" (1969)

Jimi gave the original Woodstock Nation its own anthem with this scorched-earth, Technicolor reimagining of America's theme song. Bombs bursting in air, indeed.

BAND OF GYPSYS (1970)

Jam bands in search of inspiration need look no further than this.

"BELLY BUTTON WINDOW" (1971)

This eerie, bluesy meditation on birth and reincarnation gained added poignancy by being released shortly after Hendrix's death.

tom
Cruise

52

**SIMPLY
THE BEST**

RISKY BUSINESS
(1983)
A star is born: He dances in his undies and fights Guido the killer pimp, and it doesn't deep-six his career.

RAIN MAN (1988)
An actor is born. The first definitive proof that behind Cruise's handsome smirk there is substance.

BORN ON THE
FOURTH OF JULY
(1989)
An explosive portrayal of a paralyzed Vietnam vet won him a Best Actor nod.

JERRY MAGUIRE
(1996)
"You complete me." This romance is all gooey, but it's also undeniably tear-jerking stuff. Why fight it?

MAGNOLIA (1999)
The ego has landed—it was a delicious jolt to see the actor so affectingly tap into this send-up of the macho male animal.

He could have been just another brat packer, coasting along on his 500-watt smile, playing air guitar in his undies for the rest of his career. Or he might have been content to remain an action figure, filling his résumé with blow-dried race-car drivers and jet pilots. But what makes Tom Cruise a great actor—as well as a box office champ—is that he never stopped trying to make himself better, never stopped pushing himself to go farther than where he's been.

More than any other actor of his generation, Cruise has selected his projects—and, more important, his directors—with an unerring eye toward self-improvement, seasoning his unmatched commercial success with equal portions of artistic achievement. Martin Scorsese, Oliver Stone, Barry Levinson, Stanley Kubrick—Cruise has been tutored by the best, and each teacher has tweaked his craft to surprising new heights. "He's like an animal for information," says Paul Thomas Anderson (*Boogie Nights*), who directed Cruise in 1999's *Magnolia*. "He was always asking questions. Really interesting, technical stuff about what sort of lens I was using, or what I was thinking when I wrote a particular scene. He's ferociously curious."

According to Cruise, 37, that's what the gig is all about: "The fun for me is to help a director who has a strong vision service that vision. Sometimes it can be pretty horrible. You're making a hideous fool of yourself on camera. But you've got to do it. So it's important that you trust the director. You've got to pick your directors carefully."

So far, he's been picky in all the right ways—and it's taken him farther than that dazzling smile ever could. —B S

dustin
Hoffman

SHORT LEGS, BIG NOSE, OVERBITE, ODD WALK, VERY ODD RUN. Through the mid-'60s, these were characteristics bound to keep you off Hollywood's leading-man list. Then Mike Nichols plucked Dustin Hoffman from Off Broadway to star in *The Graduate* (at 30!). The flick's huge grosses exploded the pretty-boy policy, kicking open doors for guys who weren't WASPy (the likes of Woody Allen, Jack Nicholson, and Al Pacino piled right in).

Freed from the obligation to look identical in every picture, Hoffman radically mixed up his voice, his hair, his gait. He went greasy for street rat Enrico "Ratso" Rizzo in *Midnight Cowboy* (immortalizing the urban rant "I'm walkin' heah!"), put on old-coot makeup as the honorary Indian in *Little Big Man*, and went the spectacled route in *Straw Dogs*. In *Tootsie*, playing an unemployed actor who becomes a soap star in drag,

Hoffman pulled off sustained miracles in wigs and heels. "Dustin went out to restaurants as Dorothy Michaels, to test it," says the film's director Sydney Pollack. "People didn't recognize him. He also got in an elevator with José Ferrer and I don't know whether he literally grabbed José's balls, but I know he propositioned him and embarrassed the hell out of him." Some directors consider Hoffman a bit of a testicle tweaker on the set as well, and winning two Best Actor Oscars (for his roles as a divorced father in *Kramer vs. Kramer* and an autistic in *Rain Man*) evidently helped turn his arduous preparation process into an exasperatingly tortured affair. But as Hoffman, 62, told EW in 1998, "I come from the theater. And in the theater, you rehearse. I love to work on a piece." Considering the always provocative results, we're convinced. —S D

53

SIMPLY THE BEST	THE GRADUATE (1967)	MIDNIGHT COWBOY (1969)	LITTLE BIG MAN (1970)	TOOTSIE (1982)	HOOK (1991)
	Has anybody made sexual discomfort funnier than he does in the seduction scene with Anne Bancroft?	He put pebbles in his shoe to get his limp—and a lump in audiences' throats in the tender death scene.	As a white honorary Indian stumbling through the Wild West, he makes every moment work.	His transformation into Dorothy Michaels ranks with Jack Lemmon's in *Some Like It Hot* in the drag-comedy hall of fame.	An overproduced wince inducer, but Hoffman's note-perfect turn as the pirate captain is tremendously engaging comedy.

SIMPLY THE BEST

HUNKY DORY (1971)
Explores his favorite themes: mutation ("Changes"), fabulous hauteur ("Queen Bitch"), and space ("Life on Mars?")

THE RISE AND FALL OF ZIGGY STARDUST AND THE SPIDERS FROM MARS (1972)
A rocking concept album about an alien pop star!?

STATION TO STATION (1976)
It feels like a sweeping, six-song ode to the aristocracy. Debauched and doomed.

LOW (1977)
Desolation has never sounded so sumptuous. (Wallow in the lush darkness of "Weeping Wall" and "Subterraneans.")

LET'S DANCE (1983)
Fluffy? So what. *Dance* was his most mainstream enterprise, but it perfectly bottled the sweet fizz of the Reagan boom.

54
david
Bowie

DAVID BOWIE IS THE SUPREME INCARNATION OF THE adage, "He was X before X was cool." He was gender-bending before gender-bending was cool. He was a tech whiz before tech was cool. He was heavily into space aliens before space aliens were cool. Crooner, songwriter, actor, out-and-proud gay man, straight married man, art-gallery bohemian, Internet entrepreneur, fashionista, and the guy who basically created the creepy-aristo glamour that's come to define English rock stardom, Bowie, 53, is above all a Nobel laureate in the science of staying ahead of the curve.

"The thing I always really wanted was creative success—to have albums that I could look back on and say, 'Well, that was an important album, whether or not anybody else knows it,'" he told EW in 1997. Take *Low*, the chilly requiem of alienation that Bowie cut with Brian Eno in 1977—and whose eerie chromosomal code can be detected in the likes of Nine Inch Nails and Radiohead. "At the time, it received incredibly hostile press," Bowie said. "But that's now turned into one of the milestone albums that I made."

Like Madonna, the fan who ushered him into the Rock and Roll Hall of Fame, Bowie is a maestro of metamorphosis. (If his image is plastic, so is his music: Infectious songs like "Ziggy Stardust," "Let's Dance," "Panic in Detroit," "Ashes to Ashes," "Golden Years," and "Life on Mars?" always seemed to come from some freaky synthetic kitchen where cheesy ingredients such as disco, glam, techno, and cabaret were as tasty as rock's meat-and-potatoes stock, country and blues.) "Consistency," Oscar Wilde wrote, "is the last refuge of the unimaginative." From that vantage point, Bowie has been drastically, magnificently inconsistent. Whether you're talking about his hair or his hemline, count on nothing—except his ability to keep you guessing. —JG

THIS IS THE MARK OF THE POWER OF THE BEACH BOYS' early music: that after all their well-publicized lawsuits, divorces, drugs, deaths, and breakdowns, we can still put on "Help Me, Rhonda" or *Pet Sounds*, let all that accumulated knowledge fall away, and be rendered happily, helplessly teenage. With richly textured pop that's been described as a cross between the Four Freshmen and Tchaikovsky, mercurial visionary Brian Wilson raised everyday adolescent longing to almost absurd levels of sublimity. The earliest singles, like "Surfin' U.S.A.," presented a perfect illusion of California froth to an envious, fun-craving nation. But soon Wilson was working with scores of musicians on increasingly dense, sometimes melancholy masterpieces. And unlike fellow wall-of-sound builder Phil Spector, "he brought his own music in," recalls Carol

55

Kaye, who played bass or guitar on virtually all the group's '60s sessions. "It wasn't written out very well—he had stems on the wrong sides of the notes because he wasn't very educated—but he heard things symphonically and wrote classically. We never saw the rest of the guys before they put their vocals down, except when they'd come in for a minute or two and listen to the track." Crafting his expansive *Pet* sound in early '66, Brian Wilson was challenged by the Beatles' *Rubber Soul*, and Paul McCartney has said in turn, "I sort of directed [*Sgt.*] *Pepper*. And my influence was basically the *Pet Sounds* album." What a contest! Unfortunately, a troubled Brian turned on and then dropped out, while the rest of the group undertook a three-decade run largely on the nostalgia circuit. But oh, those moments in the sun. —CW

the
Beach Boys

SIMPLY THE BEST	"IN MY ROOM" (1963)	"I GET AROUND" (1964)	"GOOD VIBRA-TIONS" (1966)	*PET SOUNDS* (1966)	*SMILE* (CIRCA 1967)
	In the midst of surf, they made this testament to turf—home turf—and a teen's room as a cocoon.	This early single perfectly expresses the quintessential exaltation of adolescent freedom.	Brian Wilson's crowning virtuosic accomplishment: a symphony in under four minutes	The saddest masterpiece of the go-go '60s, *Pet* proved that Wilson "just wasn't made for these times," but for the ages.	Never completed, this Holy Grail of lost albums exists only in our imaginations—or as teasing fragments from bootleggers.

jerry
Seinfeld

FOR A COMEDIAN WHOSE REVOLUTIONARY SITCOM REVELED IN the tiny annoyances that added up to big headaches in '90s urban life, Jerry Seinfeld is, reports friend and colleague Larry Charles, remarkably free of angst. "It's kind of scary how unneurotic he was," says the *Dilbert* exec producer of his days writing for *Seinfeld*. "His neurosis was his lack of neuroses. It was uncanny that he seemed so okay. He doesn't look back or forward; he's not hung up on where he's going or where he's been."

As a seasoned comic of the observational, sock-lost-in-the-dryer school, Seinfeld made a nice living and told a good joke. But with *Seinfeld*—in which four maladjusted single New Yorkers lived desperate lives of little importance without ever learning from their mistakes—the comedian, working with series cocreator Larry David, forever expanded the possibilities of the sitcom form; you can

56

still see the spawn of Jerry, Elaine, George, and Kramer all over the dial two years after the last episode aired. That the series helped NBC retain its first-place ranking wasn't lost on the network honchos who begged the star to keep going for one last, 10th season. But even though he loved the job (Charles interprets Seinfeld's smiley line readings as meaning "I'm having a great time! I know I'm in a TV show! Isn't this funny?!"), and probably the money, too (a million an episode), the comedian, now 46, was wise enough to know when enough was enough.

"He never let fame affect his daily life," says Charles. "He wanted that daily, normal life—to walk down the street, to get coffee." Jerry the character may have clung to his psychic tics and follies, but Jerry the entertainer turns out to have had a sane sense of the difference between man and Superman. —LS

SIMPLY THE BEST

"THE CHINESE RESTAURANT" (MAY 23, 1991)
Pick just four *Seinfeld*s? Get out. Still, this real-time episode makes Seinfeldian nothingness an art form.

"THE CONTEST" (NOV. 18, 1992)
No sitcom has ever mined an X-rated topic—being master of your domain— for such poetic hilarity.

"THE SOUP NAZI" (NOV. 2, 1995)
The fab foursome are willing to withstand wildly funny abuse just to get some really good soup.

"THE YADA YADA" (APRIL 24, 1997)
Seinfeld's prodigious ability to juggle characters and story lines reaches an apex in this classic. Yada, yada...

AMERICAN EXPRESS COMMERCIALS (DEBUTED 1992)
The man who lacked nothing pitching the card that buys everything.

stanley Kubrick

MAYBE IT WAS THE PRESSURE OF A DEADLINE BREATHING down their necks, but when Stanley Kubrick died in his sleep at the age of 70 in 1999, the chorus of obit writers and film critics sang one tune: the ballad of cinema's iciest auteur. Whether riffing on the Bronx, N.Y., native's chilly characters, robotic technical perfectionism, sterile violence, or hermetic personal life, the eulogizing horde avoided, dismissed, or completely ignored the vital and human warmth that courses through Kubrick's 13 feature films.

Steven Spielberg, arguably the most emotional of modern directors, immediately saw the heart beating within Kubrick's work. "While a lot of critics were decrying the lack of humanity in *2001: A Space Odyssey*, as a college student I was moved to tears watching it. I thought its effort to be cold was exactly what made it so personal and kind of tragic," he says. "Kubrick was probably the greatest technical craftsman ever, but I think he also made very emotional movies. Look at *Lolita* and *Full Metal Jacket*."

Or better yet, take a look at his classic 1957 WWI film, *Paths of Glory*. That movie contains one of the most powerful examples of the director's deep-rooted humanity. Kirk Douglas' French troops, just returning from the front, visit a café. A terrified German woman is pushed to the stage, where she musters the courage to sing a folk song. As the audience hoots and hollers, the film cuts to their faces, which slowly, nearly imperceptibly, move from raucous catcalls to bewildered compassion to tears. In a few moments, Kubrick's laid bare the horrors of war and the redemption found in forgiveness. "He went out of his way to tell emotional stories—he just wasn't willing to sentimentalize," says Spielberg. "As I've grown older, I've tried to learn that from him." —CN

57

SIMPLY THE BEST

THE KILLING (1956)
If you think Tarantino invented fractured, non-linear storytelling, check out this early black-and-white heist flick.

SPARTACUS (1960)
Kirk Douglas stars as a slave-turned-gladiator-turned-freedom-fighter-and-martyr. Each frame is a visual bacchanalia.

DR. STRANGELOVE (1964)
Ballsy, brash, and hilarious, Kubrick's dead-on political satire cuts Cold War America to the quick.

A CLOCKWORK ORANGE (1971)
Some thought it was trying to make ultraviolent nihilism hip, but it's really a tale about free will.

FULL METAL JACKET (1987)
The first half hour is the most haunting descent into madness ever caught on celluloid.

THE SONNY AND CHER COMEDY HOUR (1971–74)

Sonny's better half raised eyebrows with her ensembles, but it was her voice and comedic talent that made the variety show a hit.

SILKWOOD (1983)

Her turn as a tough, lesbian nuclear-power-plant worker was a first attempt at serious acting. She managed to upstage star Meryl Streep and earned an Oscar nomination.

MASK (1985)

Despite on-set tension, Cher's performance as a carefree biker chick fiercely loyal to her disabled son (played by Eric Stoltz) earned her more critical raves.

▲ MOONSTRUCK (1987)

Finally, a statuette. As an Italian-American widow who falls head over heels for her fiancé's baker brother (Nicolas Cage), Cher took home the Best Actress Oscar.

BELIEVE (1999)

She may have been 53, but this album's infectious dance tunes were heard at clubs around the world, making a believer out of anyone who ever doubted her career longevity.

Cher

114   PHOTOGRAPH BY STEVE SCHAPIRO

FAME IS A MICROSCOPE. THE CRUSHING ADULATION THAT COMES with celebrity has laid low many a star. But that rubric never applied to Cher. For her, fame was/is/always will be a kaleidoscope. Train your gaze on Cher at any point in her career, and just as you begin to resolve one spectacular, oversaturated vision of her, she turns your focus, letting another multihued shard of her personality fall into view. Suddenly you're staring at another image—an intriguingly fresh image, but still singular, bright, bigger than life. Still Cher.

58

See her in the '60s: the exotic, beautiful half of Sonny and Cher, a sweet hippie couple who sing poppy hits. Look again in the '70s: There she is, ultraglam TV vixen on *The Sonny and Cher Comedy Hour*, a wry straight woman in outrageous showgirl clothing. Turn your attention to the '80s: Now she's an actress stealing scenes from Meryl Streep(!) in 1983's *Silkwood*, and she walks away with the 1987 Best Actress Oscar for *Moonstruck*. By the '90s, she's in her full hyper-speed mode, by turns a hair-care pitchwoman, a mail-order catalog entrepreneur, a touching eulogist (for ex-husband Sonny Bono), and a blue-haired dance club diva.

"She got handed more lives than the rest of us," says her *Comedy Hour* designer Bob Mackie. A fair appraisal, but Cher, 54, has always known that she's lived one life—it's just had many angles. "Hollywood doesn't think I'm part of it," she once said. "Neither does the music business. Somehow I manage." And because she always will, we happily peer through the kaleidoscope once more. —SM

Prince

PRINCE IS 2 weird 4 HIS OWN GOOD. THERE ARE THE BIZARRE name changes (♀), the record-label battles, the word *slave* on his cheek. He annulled his marriage to wife Mayte because he doesn't trust contracts. He's rerecording his entire catalog so he can own the master tapes. The man born Prince Rogers Nelson is stubborn, eccentric, idealistic, proud, sincere, and spiritual. He loves God and sex and music and isn't ashamed of whatever impulses all three arouse in him. These are good qualities. But somewhere between Paisley Park, his Minnesota recording complex, and the outside world, the 42-year-old's personality gets muddled and misinterpreted, making him seem only slightly less freakish than Michael Jackson.

But here's the thing: Behind all the eccentricity is a breathtaking talent. A prodigy who put out his first album when he was 19, he is among contemporary music's most accomplished songwriters, penning as many of the last two decades' great songs as anyone: "1999" and "When Doves Cry," to name just two. A true studio wizard, he spent the early '80s crafting a distinctive combination of screaming guitar, loose-limbed funk, and futuristic electronics, both on his own records and on those of protégés like Sheila E. While recording, he often plays every instrument himself. And live? There is no more arousing performer. "Here's a guy who's made some of the most incredible records of the last I don't know how many years—and he's still innocent whenever he picks up a guitar," says singer-songwriter Ani DiFranco, who worked on Prince's upcoming album. "After a while celebrity becomes a weight, and it's hard to be reinspired every day. But he shines every time." —RB

59

SIMPLY THE BEST

DIRTY MIND (1980)
From the racy cover to the unabashed "Do It All Night" and "Head," this is a sexually raw and musically refined early triumph.

1999 (1982)
Perfecting the formula of funky filth and commercial pop that would make him a star, he mixes sweaty jams with tight songcraft.

PURPLE RAIN (1984)
Smutty ("Darling Nikki"), sweet ("I Would Die 4 U"), and soulful ("Purple Rain"). Skip the awful film.

"KISS" (1986)
Prince's cooing falsetto drove this perfectly simple funk throwback up to the top of the charts.

SIGN O' THE TIMES (1987)
Features some of his best pop songs, like "If I Was Your Girlfriend" and "Ballad of Dorothy Parker."

SIMPLY THE BEST

▲ *RED HEADED STRANGER* (1975)
As authentic as old rope and barbed wire, and as close as you'll get to sitting around a tumbleweed campfire with a troop of Old West cowpokes

WILLIE AND FAMILY LIVE (1978)
Willie at the dizzy peak of his rowdy phase, hootin' and moanin' about whiskey rivers and Bloody Mary mornings

STARDUST (1978)
Like Louis Armstrong and Frank Sinatra, Willie became a classic by making the classics his own. Gasp at the way his parched tenor crawls through "Georgia on My Mind."

THIEF (1981)
Watch for Willie's small but heart-crushing performance in this heist flick directed by Michael Mann.

▲ *TEATRO* (1998)
Produced by Daniel Lanois, *Teatro* is a spooky, flamenco-tinged look back at lost love and instant karma.

PHOTOGRAPH BY MARY ELLEN MARK

60
willie
Nelson

IT'S HARD TO IMAGINE, BUT WILLIE NELSON—INFAMOUS target of the Internal Revenue Service, frank evangelist for the pacifying effects of marijuana, a guy instantly identified by a flappin'-in-the-breeze ponytail and a scraggly veld of facial hair—once did a stint in the United States Air Force. It was decades ago, when he was a young farm boy from rural Texas, and it didn't last very long. "I'm just one of those guys who is *not* cut out for military service," Nelson told EW in 1998. "I don't take directions very well." After just eight months, a medical discharge eased him out of the *Top Gun* career path—and started him on the potholed road to Nashville. "I had a back injury," the singer explains with a conspiratorial wink, "and it was a very convenient one."

Therein lies Willie Nelson's appeal—and his subtly radical impact on American culture: The man's life is a study in the high art of *gettin' away with it.* Yep, his musical career is rhinestoned with breathtaking accomplishments. He wrote classics like "Crazy" and "Hello Walls." He confounded and changed Nashville by cutting a series of albums—from 1975's sweeping *Red Headed Stranger* to 1998's spectral *Teatro*—that shocked country music back to its outlaw roots. (And, paradoxically, he turned twang into a gold rush with 1978's *Stardust*, a mega-platinum phenom.) For a while, thanks to the chuggin'-down-the-highway charm of 1980's *Honeysuckle Rose*, he even became a movie star. But in the end, the résumé pales next to his message, the hard-earned wisdom you hear in his soothing vibrato: With enough spirit, even your darkest mistakes can yield glimmers of grace. It's a lesson Nelson, 67, knows firsthand. "If I was put here to write songs," he muses, "then I was damn sure going to have to experience life." —JG

jim
Henson

IN THE '60S, JIM HENSON USED TO TAKE HIS MUPPETEERING partner, Frank Oz, to see avant-garde shorts by Andy Warhol and Stan Brakhage. "I wasn't that impressed," remembers Oz. "He always said, 'Yeah, maybe 90 percent isn't good, but you can learn from the other 10 percent.' He always wanted to be a serious filmmaker."

Indeed, Henson—who was nominated for an Oscar in 1965 for his short *Time Piece*—turned his sights to puppetry in the '50s only as a way to infiltrate TV: A Washington, D.C., program wanted puppet acts, so he chopped up a green coat and called it Kermit. By the time the Muppets exploded the concept of children's TV with *Sesame Street* in 1969, Henson's fate was sealed. In the showbiz satire *The Muppet Show* or features like *The Great Muppet Caper*, his cuddly stars mocked our human foibles mercilessly—and we couldn't get enough. "My father's approach to life was, If it gets frustrating, laugh at the absurdity," says Brian Henson, who took over the Jim Henson Co. after his dad died, at age 53, in 1990. "He captured that energy with the Muppets."

61

Yet he didn't neglect the experimentalist within, whether it was procuring one of the first Moog synthesizers to score a *Sesame Street* segment or filming the seemingly unfilmable (e.g., Miss Piggy's swimming in *Caper*, for which Henson had Oz submerged with bricks on his feet). How would Henson assess his legacy? "He'd be proud of having come so far," muses Muppeteer Jerry Juhl. "But he'd be wishing he'd done more." He wouldn't be the only one. —KRISTEN BALDWIN

SIMPLY THE BEST	**"SAM AND FRIENDS" (1955–61)**	**SESAME STREET (DEBUTED 1969)**	**THE MUPPET SHOW (1976–81)**	**THE MUPPET MOVIE (1979)**	**FRAGGLE ROCK (1983–88)**
	"Hi ho!" Viewers were introduced to Kermit the Frog on this local Washington, D.C., puppet program.	Thanks to his Muppets, learning the ABC's is a lot more fun—especially with a monster named Grover.	235 million viewers in over 100 countries tuned in weekly to see who Statler and Waldorf would insult.	A celeb-packed triumph of comedy (have you tried Hare Krishna?) and technology (Kermit rides a bike!)	Leaving Kermit and Co. behind, he created a world of whimsical creatures for this much-feted HBO series.

warren Beatty

WATCH WARREN BEATTY'S FILMS AND YOU'LL notice a pattern: The guy *dies* a lot. His characters tend to croak prematurely, in the midst of chasing some mad dream. Whether it's Jack Reed's Communist ideal in *Reds*, a gangster's Vegas fantasia in *Bugsy*, a drifter's crime spree in *Bonnie and Clyde*, or a U.S. senator's last-ditch epiphany of truth telling and rapping in *Bulworth*, the hero's ultimate reward is gruesome expiration. "It's something we're *all* gonna do," Beatty, 63, demurs. "Everybody feels they die prematurely." But those films share something else, too. They're impossible to imagine apart from the passion of another American dreamer: Beatty.

62

There's a scene in *Reds* when Reed, an American writer who's joined the Communist cause, gets into an argument with a Russian propagandist who's sugarcoated his speech. "He can't abide the censorship of his telling of the truth," explains Beatty. "It's that conflict between politics and art in Reed that's very dramatic." In Beatty, too. A man of staggering physical beauty, he nevertheless used his charisma to make some of the truest and boldest films in Hollywood. "It's a mistake not to do what interests you," says Beatty. "I've been able to do what I wanted. I spent time in politics. I've had my share of fun." Which leads to the perfect epitaph—or campaign slogan. "I don't regret anything I've done," he says. "You regret what you *don't* do." —JG

jodie Foster

63

AT 3, SHE WAS BRINGING HOME A PAYCHECK AS A Coppertone baby. At 13, she was playing a prostitute on movie screens nationwide. At 18, seeking peaceful semi-anonymity as a college freshman, she saw her name splattered across front pages as the obsession of a would-be presidential assassin.

Stories that begin this way, with child stardom and precociousness and scandal, are supposed to end this way: drugs. Arrests. Failed comebacks. Plaintive appearances on *Maury Povich*. Instead, Jodie Foster's story goes this way: Academy Award. Directing gig. Producing job. Second Academy Award. New baby. $15 million paycheck. Respect of entire movie industry. Hints of more greatness to come.

Foster has made a career of defying expectations. As a child actress, she was less interested in appearing adorable than in sharing the screen with Robert De Niro in *Taxi Driver*. She startled people in an industry defined by ambition by spending four years at Yale, then startled them again by playing a working-class rape victim in *The Accused* (Oscar No. 1), then yet again by holding her own against Anthony Hopkins in *The Silence of the Lambs* (Oscar No. 2). And, in a business where valuing your privacy means going on *Entertainment Tonight* to complain about how horrible it is that the media won't leave you and Gwyneth alone, Foster does something almost incomprehensible: She lives a private life.

This is why we love Foster: because she has standards, intelligence, and a willingness to take chances. She gives unsulky interviews about what she does for a living. Her inspiration: "I look at my family's lives, because they're the people I'm close to," says Foster, 37. "Not that I do imitations of them. It's more a process of getting interested in why people are what they are." Foster has done her job well. Whenever she comes to play, we are always, always interested. —DAVE KARGER

SIMPLY THE BEST

BONNIE AND CLYDE (1967)
Critics recall its violence, but we remember the film's hazy nonchalance—that seductive sense of peace.

McCABE AND MRS. MILLER (1971)
Robert Altman's grimy, frostbitten parable of how the West was lost

SHAMPOO (1975)
Here Beatty, one of the smartest men in Hollywood, plays dumb. He's a tower-haired himbo with a leonine libido.

REDS (1981)
Beatty wrote, produced, directed, and starred in this grand epic. It won him his only Oscar, Best Director.

BUGSY (1991)
James Toback's piercing script and Beatty's killer performance conspire to make gangster Bugsy Siegel's vanity seem heroic.

SIMPLY THE BEST

TAXI DRIVER (1976)
Her lived-in, Oscar-nominated turn as a preteen prostitute proved she wasn't just any kiddie actor.

THE ACCUSED (1988)
The first of two Best Actress Academy Awards honored her performance as a righteous and vulnerable rape victim.

LITTLE MAN TATE (1991)
She protected her gifted son—and beautifully showed her maternal instincts. She also directed.

THE SILENCE OF THE LAMBS (1991)
Clarice Starling, her most indelible character, provided Foster with a daring role—and an Oscar.

NELL (1994)
Her gibberish-spouting backwoods free spirit required much courage and resulted in Foster's personal favorite performance.

joni
Mitchell

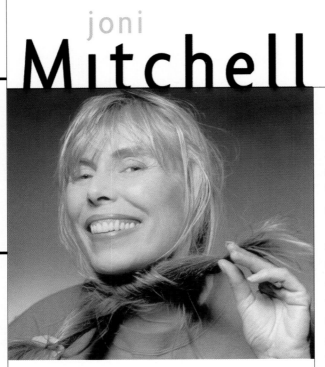

WHO KNEW, WHEN JONI MITCHELL WAS FIRST melting folk-rock hearts with sense-of-wonder songs like "Chelsea Morning," that behind the sweet soprano lay popular music's most stubborn personality, a woman who would consistently veer from the expected path? The Canadian's late-'60s arrival came at a time when "women's songs were written by men, 99 percent of the time. They carried the old feminine values according to the master," Mitchell, 56, remembers. "My songs began to reveal feminine insecurities, doubts, recognition that the order was falling apart." The abundance of songs on the confessional standard-setter *Blue* led to her most successful album, 1974's *Court and Spark*. And right at that commercial peak, our Lady of the Canyon took another ravine less traveled: the way of Miles and Mingus. "I stopped playing in standard tuning, to get chords that didn't sound like the chords everybody else was playing. In the same way that Van Gogh searched for his own color schemes, I searched for my own harmonic voice, found it, and spent a career being dismissed as too jazzy." Resistance only stiffened her resolve. "Black influence on my work seemed to offend young white critics," she laughs. "When *Hejira* [1976] was trashed in America, I thought, there's nothing to do except experiment more." Mitchell's albums continue to mine this uncompromising vein, empowering devotees from Tori Amos to Prince. Most laudably, Mitchell never used her rare tours to milk the oldies, unlike any middle-aged contemporary you'd care to name. "I will not be a living jukebox," she declares. "I tried to make that very clear along the way." Crystal. —CW

IF IT WERE UP TO DAVID LETTERMAN, HIS TENURE as a talk-show host would be summed up thusly: "I always wanted to be Johnny Carson. Sadly, I'm not, and I prove it every night of the week."

He's nothing if not consistent. Letterman has made a career of playing the insecure underdog—to brilliant effect: Just as there was indeed only one Carson, there will be only one late-night host who so deftly punctured the bubble of showbiz convention (though now he's in a double-breasted suit). A former TV weatherman who once congratulated a tropical storm on being upgraded to hurricane status, Letterman raised smarmy-pants irony to high art and, in the process, recast the late-show persona (see Conan O'Brien, Craig Kilborn, and Jon Stewart). Before Letterman, there was no shameless slagging of network bosses, no tossing of melons off rooftops, no celebration of tomfoolery (absurdist skits like "May we press your pants, please?") and frat-boy stupidity (animal or otherwise). "What attracted me to Dave was that he was going by his own compass," says O'Brien, who inherited Letterman's NBC time slot when Dave moved to CBS in '93. "This wasn't a slick operation. He wasn't trying to win you over. He was doing things *he* thought were funny."

And if they weren't? Even better. Letterman's tendency to turn his struggle for Carson-like perfection into self-flagellation produces comic gold. "Show business was always about pretending everything's great, everybody's putting on a show," says Rob Barnett, *Letterman* exec producer. "Here comes this guy who tells you exactly what's going on, because it's the only way he knows how to behave. If he's cranky, he's cranky. When things don't go well, he'll turn around and say, 'Boy, does this *stink*!'" It's what you'd call the sweet smell of success. —DS

david
Letterman

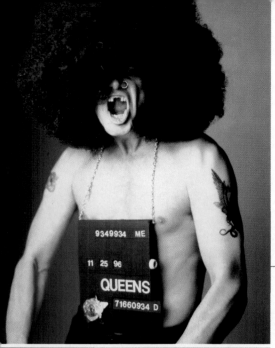

66

jim
Carrey

"I'M SO NOT THE FUNNIEST MAN IN AMERICA," insists Chris Rock, who got that title from TIME. "Jim Carrey is. Anyone who knows anything about funny knows that Jim is the funniest man in the world."

But why? Does it have to do with those childishly zany body contortions? Or those irrepressibly manic impressions? Or maybe a certain facility for talking out of his butt?

Here's a wacky theory: It's because of Carrey's bleak sensibility, a dark-as-sackcloth outlook on life that colors his every freaky twitch, rubbery grimace, and vocal explosion. Not seeing it? Check out his karaoke version of Jefferson Airplane's "Somebody to Love" in 1996's criminally underrated *The Cable Guy*; it's the most disturbing crooning this side of a Celine Dion concert. Look at the opening sequence of *Ace Ventura: Pet Detective*, where Carrey plays a twisted delivery guy kicking a box down a hallway like Pelé in a 'roid rage. And then there's the supposedly family-friendly *Liar Liar*, where a self-loathing Carrey beats the bejesus out of himself in a bathroom.

"He enjoys the feeling of fear," says Bobby Farrelly, who directed Carrey in both *Dumb and Dumber* and this summer's *Me, Myself & Irene*. "When he thinks something's scary, he doesn't run from it." Rather, he embraces it. From this fear and loathing, Carrey fuels his humor with the delirious energy of a man who's seen the dark side and come back to laugh, loudly and sweetly, at the demons. Perhaps it stems from his personal experiences: After all, this is a guy who lived with his homeless family in a van as a child, then spent years floundering in Hollywood. Whatever the reason, it's inspired in Carrey a relentless drive and riveting lunacy that can blow people away.

"To be near him is like being in a hurricane," says Farrelly. "It exhausts you." And sometimes, when you're done laughing, it scares you, just a bit. —AJJ

aaron Spelling

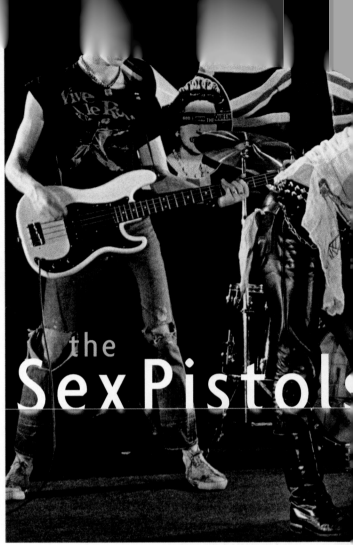

the SexPistols

NONE OF AARON SPELLING'S 57 SERIES HAS EVER WON TOP honors at the Emmys. Just his name alone evokes images of fluffy, hairstyle TV. He's also responsible for *Models, Inc.* But guess what? *None of that matters.* Critics be damned: Spelling is still television's most accessible, prolific, and downright entertaining raconteur. "He is one of the greatest short-story tellers of all time," says longtime producing partner E. Duke Vincent. "He has the ability to consistently read what the public wants to see and then give it to them."

Ever since abandoning a short-lived acting career in the '50s, Spelling has provided us with the tube's most enticing trends. Case in point: He predicted the teen movement some 30 years before everyone else (see 1968's *The Mod Squad*), having long pondered Hollywood's neglect of that audience. "My mother and I used to walk to the theater every Saturday," says the producer, now 72. "I was 12 or 13, and there was never anything for me to see."

Building on *Mod*'s success, Spelling forged prime-time TV's templates, with '70s escapist romps (*Charlie's Angels, Fantasy Island*), '80s Reaganomics melodrama (*Dynasty, Hotel*), and '90s youth obsession (*Melrose Place, Beverly Hills, 90210*). It wasn't all glitz; Spelling also showcased social issues, as in two Emmy-winning telefilms: 1988's antinuke drama *Day One* and 1992's *And the Band Played On*, one of TV's first looks at AIDS. "It was the hardest thing I've ever done," says Spelling of *Band*'s four-year odyssey to the screen. "I'm terribly proud of that."

Spelling currently exec-produces five shows—including The WB's top-rated *7th Heaven*—and plans to extend his empire into the millennium. "I once said a stupid thing, that I like doing cotton candy for the mind," Spelling sighs. "I'll *never* live that down." Perhaps not, but at least he's made cotton candy a legitimate TV food group. —K B

57

68

SIMPLY THE BEST

THE MOD SQUAD (1968–73) Spelling proved shows about teens were all right for TV with this drama featuring a trio of hippie cops.

CHARLIE'S ANGELS (1976–81) The clothes! The camp! The cans of hair spray used on Farrah's feathered 'do! He introduces us to jiggle TV.

DYNASTY (1981–89) Viewers loved watching rich folks behaving badly. With eight Spelling shows on in 1981, ABC was called "Aaron's Broadcasting Co."

SIMPLY THE BEST

ELVIS PRESLEY (1957 Would the King's sexy swivel hips corrupt viewers The straight-arrow host nervously let millions enjo Elvis—from the waist up.

DID THE SEX PISTOLS—HEADLINE-GRABBING HOOLIGANS WHOSE whole career lasted a few mad months—invent punk rock? Nope. But who cares? More than the Ramones or the Clash, they punctured the prim, the pompous, and Pink Floyd with naughty expulsions of noise. They reminded the world how to heckle. Today, their shock-sarcasm pops up everywhere from *South Park* to Howard Stern. "People wanted to see them buried alive," says Julien Temple, who directed *The Filth and the Fury*, a recent documentary about the band. "But what they were castigated for is normal now."

In the '70s, most folks missed the point. "They thought it was like a show," says Pistols guitarist Steve Jones, 44, "like going to see Kiss or something." Prudes scowled at the "rage" in songs like "Anarchy in the U.K.," but savvy listeners got their real sting: Snaggletoothed frontman Johnny Rotten was the most hilarious provocateur since Lenny Bruce. "Their attack was in their comedy," says Temple. "Although they shocked, there was a great sense of humor to it."

Prodded along by manager Malcolm McLaren, the Pistols didn't just poke fun at the Queen, they deflated *themselves*. They cut an entire album casting the band as a loony fraud: *The Great Rock 'N' Roll Swindle* features a cheesy Eurodisco medley of their own hits, foul scraps of pirate doggerel and vaudeville, and Frank Sinatra's signature psalm, "My Way," as pulverized by downward-spiral poster boy Sid Vicious. "That was very much the point," says Temple, "that nothing was really sacred, that rock & roll was meant to be irreverent. It was a tremendously refreshing thing at the time." It still is. —JG

ed Sullivan

HE LOOKED AS LUGUBRIOUS AS AN UNDERTAKER AND MOVED with the ease of Richard Nixon on a tense day. But if Ed Sullivan, a shy showbiz gossip columnist and host of his own TV variety hour for 23 years, didn't know how to swing himself, he had a talent for spotting people who did. And he wasn't afraid to mix them up on his "really big shew," whether they were ambassadors of high culture, pop culture, or something as off the cultural charts as a puppet called Topo Gigio.

Sullivan's stiff mannerisms and frequently mangled attempts at emcee cheerleading (*"Let's hear it for the Lord's Prayer!"*) were regularly lampooned by comedians. But his open-minded embrace of the new as well as the old was admired and influential—as was his support of African-American performers, from Sammy Davis Jr. and Bill

"Bojangles" Robinson to Stevie Wonder and James Brown. "[Sullivan] was a very smart man and knew he needed them as much as they needed him," says singer and frequent guest Eddie Fisher, recalling that "being on Ed Sullivan could make you." Of the more than 10,000 performers who took the stage of *The Ed Sullivan Show* (called *The Toast of the Town* until 1955), some, like the Beatles, forever changed music. Some, like Richard Pryor, forever changed stand-up comedy. And some, like the dancing elephants and circus artists Sullivan doted on, preserved the tradition of the variety show as family fun, the logical extension of the host's formula: "Open big, have a good comedy act, put in something for children, and keep the show clean."

When he died of cancer in 1974 at 73, his show had been off the air for three years, a casualty of cresting TV hipness. Yet unspool an old episode today, and it's not retro nostalgia that captivates; it's the unjaded tastes of a man as unfazed by hipness as by elephants dancing on his stage. —LS

THE BEATLES (1964)	THE ROLLING STONES (1967)	SIMPLY THE BEST	NEVER MIND THE BOLLOCKS, HERE'S THE SEX PISTOLS (1977)	THE GREAT ROCK 'N' ROLL SWINDLE (1979)	SID AND NANCY (1986)
Four lads from Liverpool sang two ditties—"She Loves You" and "I Want to Hold Your Hand"—and popular culture was changed forever.	Jagger changed "Let's Spend the Night Together" to "Let's Spend Some Time Together" to perform on the show.		Like a tornado, they ripped into rock city, tossed debris all over, and then vanished.	A freakish collection of odds and sods that's just as hilarious as *This Is Spiñal Tap*	Johnny Rotten hates this movie, of course, but Gary Oldman's portrayal of Sid Vicious is drooling, slurring, death-wish poetry.

steve Martin

HIS EYES GO WIDE. HIS JAW SLACKENS. DUMB ENTHUSIASM COURSES through his body and that trademark grin explodes. The startling screwball effect underscores a complex truth: No one does a smarter job of playing dim than Steve Martin.

There's been a lot of media musing lately about Martin's metamorphosis from jerk to genius, from wild and crazy guy to *New Yorker* belletrist. In fact, both Martins have always existed within his prematurely snowcapped skull. Beneath the most antic, arrow-through-the-head frenzies of yore was the mind of a coolly detached philosophy major, and grinning just under the surface of Martin's elegant essays is a lunatic jester. Still, it makes for one of Hollywood's stranger career arcs. "It started in the early '70s. I was off developing weird stuff in nightclubs where nobody was watching," remembers Martin, 54. "Really lousy, really lonely. But hey, I made the waitresses laugh."

Career shift No. 1 occurred at the peak of his stand-up fame; he abandoned it to spend the next 15 years solidifying his status as a movie star. Beginning with his breakthrough film, 1979's *The Jerk*, and continuing on through such innovative projects as *Dead Men Don't Wear Plaid* and *All of Me*, Martin established himself as the goofball intellectuals could love. But with the '90s came another shift: serious acting (*The Spanish Prisoner*) and heady humor penned for magazines and theater (the whimsical *Picasso at the Lapin Agile*). "There was nothing planned," says Martin of his various career transitions. "I stopped things because I wasn't happy doing them anymore."

"Steve got more layered," says longtime collaborator Frank Oz, who directed Martin's most recent film, *Bowfinger*. "At the beginning he was like grape juice, now he's becoming wine. I loved the grape juice, but now it goes deeper." Whatever the vintage, we'll have what he's having. —D F

paul Simon

'70

TO LISTEN TO THE MUSIC OF PAUL SIMON is to trace the steps of our national journey from innocence to irony. In the late 1960s, he was America's campus poet, the AM-radio bard for every sensitive English-lit major who'd ever daydreamed about strolling through Greenwich Village on a rainy autumn night. Even the titles of his early elegies with Art Garfunkel—"I Am a Rock," "The Sounds of Silence," "The Dangling Conversation"—sound like the tweedy strivings of a young Bleecker Street poet. Which is precisely what made Simon & Garfunkel the ideal soundtrack for Dustin Hoffman's diploma-toting fog in *The Graduate*: Lovely pop-folk fare like "Mrs. Robinson" and "Scarborough Fair" felt chaste and celestial and tender—homesick for childhood, not yet bruised by the world. "I used to watch Paul so closely in those days," Garfunkel recalls. "We'd be head to head, nose to nose, and I'd watch his lips and the way his tongue hit the top of his mouth to see where that amazing, glorious sound was coming from."

But it's Simon's sly, urbane, post-*Graduate* work—after the fling with Mrs. Robinson, after the rift with the seraph-voiced Garfunkel—that marked him as much more than a tunesmith in a black turtleneck. In the '70s and '80s we detected his quirks, wounds, and neuroses while he wrestled with aging, the anxiety of love, and the ache of divorce in "Something So Right," "50 Ways to Leave Your Lover," "Still Crazy After All These Years," and "Hearts and Bones." On albums like *Graceland* and in songs like "Mother and Child Reunion" he infused American pop with the music of the world—South African rhythms and harmonies, Caribbean ska, Peruvian flute melodies—long before multiculti became de rigueur.

His world expanded. So did ours. "What he does," says singer Sarah McLachlan of the now 58-year-old Simon, "is continually reinvent himself. Like the Beatles', his work, because it is always changing, will endure for decades." —D H

SIMPLY THE BEST

BRIDGE OVER TROUBLED WATER (1970)
The quintessential Simon & Garfunkel; the title track was their biggest hit ever.

STILL CRAZY AFTER ALL THESE YEARS (1975)
The classic '70s midlife-crisis album, featuring "50 Ways to Leave Your Lover"

HEARTS AND BONES (1983)
His least successful but most personal album covers topics from marriage to John Lennon's murder.

GRACELAND (1986)
Upbeat, colorful, and full of life, the album made South African dance music nearly an American institution.

THE RHYTHM OF THE SAINTS (1990)
He borrowed from West Africa, Brazil, and the world of zydeco, proving again his music has no bounds.

PHOTOGRAPH BY DEBORAH FEINGOLD

71

SIMPLY THE BEST	THE STAND-UP TAPES (1977–79) The madcap, banjo-playing, arrow-through-the-head-wearing prankster at his absolute best	*THE JERK* (1979) The comic's screen debut features perhaps the funniest opening line in film history ("I was born a poor black child").	*DIRTY ROTTEN SCOUNDRELS* (1988) Martin and Michael Caine make a great comedy team in Frank Oz's underrated remake of *Bedtime Story*.	*L.A. STORY* (1991) He plays a weatherman in a city where the weather never changes in this sweet, absurdist love letter to Los Angeles.	*THE SPANISH PRISONER* (1998) Playing against type, he steals the show as con artist Jimmy Dell in David Mamet's potboiler.

Cobain

72

HE WAS COOL BECAUSE, BARELY OUT OF his teens, his voice spoke of a life more weathered than his jeans. Intriguing because he flung his angst into his music like paint onto an unapologetic canvas. Misunderstood because, at the peak of his jagged fame, he took his own life. But strip away all the calamity and celebrity attached to Nirvana singer-guitarist Kurt Cobain, and you'll uncover a reason his imprint endures: He was a masterful composer, a creator of melodies so haunting and lush, so accessible, they intimidated even him. "Because he came from such a pure punk ethic, he wanted to suppress his pop sensibility, which he was a genius at," says Garbage drummer Butch Vig, who produced the band's '91 opus of disaffection, *Nevermind*. "He'd set up the guitar and start strumming something, and I'd go, 'What's that?' and then he'd step on a fuzz pedal and squash the melodic side right out of it."

No amount of distortion could mask his universal appeal, though: *Nevermind* sold 20 million copies worldwide. Rarely can we ascribe so much industry revolution to a musician whose career spanned a scant five years, but with those searing soundscapes and confessional-confrontational lyrics ("I'm so ugly/that's okay/'cause so are you"), Cobain stirred a nation mired in hair metal and plastic pop. Suddenly, spandex and imitation were out; Seattle grunge and alienation were in. Reaching people like no other musician since perhaps John Lennon, Cobain channeled a collective hurt; it was as if he alone were living it for us. "Very few artists change the course of popular history, not just popular music—of the way people think, dress, act, what's cool, what isn't cool. He came along at a moment in time when change was so necessary people didn't even realize how necessary until it actually happened," says Gary Gersh, the former Geffen exec who signed Nirvana. "Here was a guy willing to turn his skin inside out and let out all the true emotion. A lot of artists have been able to do that in spurts, but that was all Kurt knew how to do." Given his 1994 shotgun suicide at age 27, it was more than enough. —DS

SIMPLY THE BEST	"LOVE BUZZ" (1988)	*NEVERMIND* HITS NO. 1 (1992)	*MTV VIDEO MUSIC AWARDS* (1992)	*IN UTERO* (1993)	*MTV UNPLUGGED IN NEW YORK* (1994)
	Meet the band: Indie label Sub Pop releases Nirvana's first single, a loudmouth, punk-pop cover.	Grunge goes legit: Powered by alt-anthem "Smells Like Teen Spirit," their major-label debut tops the charts.	"Teen Spirit" wins twice! Cobain spats with Axl Rose! Bassist injured during rousing "Lithium"!	A sonic-melodic boom of grit and loathing, from "Serve the Servants"' dissonant splash to "All Apologies"' decaying chant	Recorded in a candlelit Manhattan studio, this mellow album serves as Cobain's eerie elegy.

PHOTOGRAPH BY JESSE FROHMAN

WHEN TOURING, MOST ROCK STARS INDULGE IN ONE OF SEVERal standard accoutrements: drugs, babes, maybe personal chefs. Not so Neil Young, as Greg Dulli learned when his band, Afghan Whigs, opened for him in 1996. At the first show, Dulli walked past a backstage room and heard "the sound of trains going 'Whoo-hoo!'" It was Young's massive Lionel train set, and, says Dulli, "it took up the whole room. It must have been someone's job just to set it up."

Like those miniature locomotives, Young chugs along after nearly 35 years, maintaining the same steady, unwavering, defiantly idiosyncratic pace. His body of work—music of fragile beauty, monolithic power, and occasional hippie jokiness, on his own or with his revolving bands and Crosby, Stills & Nash—is nothing short of astonishing. No other boomer rock star—not Dylan, not the Stones, not the ex-Beatles—has matched this son of a Canadian sportswriter for prolonged vitality. And despite what nonfans may view as limitations (that crackling whine of a voice, those seemingly rudimentary guitar chops), Young's very unpredictability (rockabilly? synthesizers? punk? country?) has kept him from growing complacent. At 54, Young has become the Mark Twain of rock—a craggy, folkloric figure restlessly striding the musical landscape.

"He's the most steadfast and resolute in his beliefs," enthuses Dulli, a fan since he bought "Heart of Gold" as a kid. "No matter what trends have come and gone, Neil Young remains." He also remains, in case you didn't know, a part owner of Lionel Trains since 1995. —DAVID BROWNE

neil
Young
73

| SIMPLY THE BEST | "MR. SOUL" (1967) With Buffalo Springfield, Young spits out a bilious commentary on fame, setting the stage for an unpredictable solo career. | AFTER THE GOLD RUSH (1970) From "Southern Man" to the meditative title song, he confronts life in the post-Woodstock decade. | TONIGHT'S THE NIGHT (1975) A ragged and frighteningly potent elegy to drugs and dead friends—exactly what the public didn't want | RUST NEVER SLEEPS (1979) As punk rages, Young reaffirms his forever-young vigor with ballads and Crazy Horse battering rams. | HARVEST MOON (1992) Billed as a belated sequel to Harvest, this autumnal collection personifies rock aging gracefully. |

michael
Crichton

ONCE, BY WAY OF BRUSHING OFF CRITICAL ATTACKS, MICHAEL Crichton invoked Jean Cocteau. "He didn't care about being noticed for his style," the novelist said of the avant-garde filmmaker. "He only wanted to be noticed for his ideas." Crichton's 12 novels—best-sellers all—positively teem with ideas. From the virology chills of *The Andromeda Strain* (1969) to the DNA thrills of *Jurassic Park* (1990), his fact-packed page-turners provoke our deepest anxieties about science and society. Accordingly, the author, 57, reportedly provokes publishing houses into first printings of 2 million copies and movie studios into forking over $8–10 million for film rights. (Why not? *Jurassic Park* made some $900 million worldwide.) Meanwhile, the Harvard Medical School grad's *ER* remains the No. 1 drama on TV. "He's a media polymath," says his editor, Knopf's Sonny Mehta. "A kind of late-20th-century Renaissance man." Style never seemed so superfluous. —TP

'74

IT'S THE DEFINING DRAMA OF THE '90S. DEFINITELY THE SPOOK-iest. But the most Byronic? "The whole premise of *The X-Files* is intrinsically romantic," argues star Gillian Anderson. "And Chris Carter is the *ultimate* romantic." Carter, who created the series in '92, doesn't cite the Romantics as an influence, but they may very well have appreciated it—if they didn't gag on the occasional sewer-dwelling fluke. Carter's coiling mythology of alien invasion and paranormal hanky-panky might have sprung from cynicism and suspicion, but it evolved through its protagonists—FBI agents Dana Scully (Anderson) and Fox Mulder (David Duchovny)—into an epic fable of passion and faith. Despite the endless warnings of "Trust no one," the soul of the show is proclaimed on Mulder's infamous poster: "I want to believe." In Mulder and Scully, Carter says he was after the most elusive of TV relationships: "Two people who cared about one another in a deep way that didn't end in easy consummation." Ironically, in realizing Carter's ideals, Duchovny and Anderson succeeded in making the most respectful of comrades look irresistibly sexy. "These are heroes whose friendship and search for truth are transcendent," says Carter. "We all want their relationship." —JJ

SIMPLY THE BEST	THE ANDROMEDA STRAIN (1969)	JURASSIC PARK (1990)	DISCLOSURE (1994)	ER (DEBUTED 1994)	AIRFRAME (1996)
	His debut (and most popular) novel is trademark Crichton: a brisk tale with propeller-head passages.	A crowd-pleasing mix of fascinating scientific detail and adrenaline about genetically resurrected dinos.	Once again displaying the uncanny ability to foresee real-life headlines, he tackles sexual harassment at a sleek Silicon Valley firm.	The series about scrappy, jargon-spewing docs sent a much-needed defibrillator shock to the then floundering state of TV dramas.	Touchstone Pictures paid $8–10 million for the rights to this mystery thriller about a suspicious plane crash.

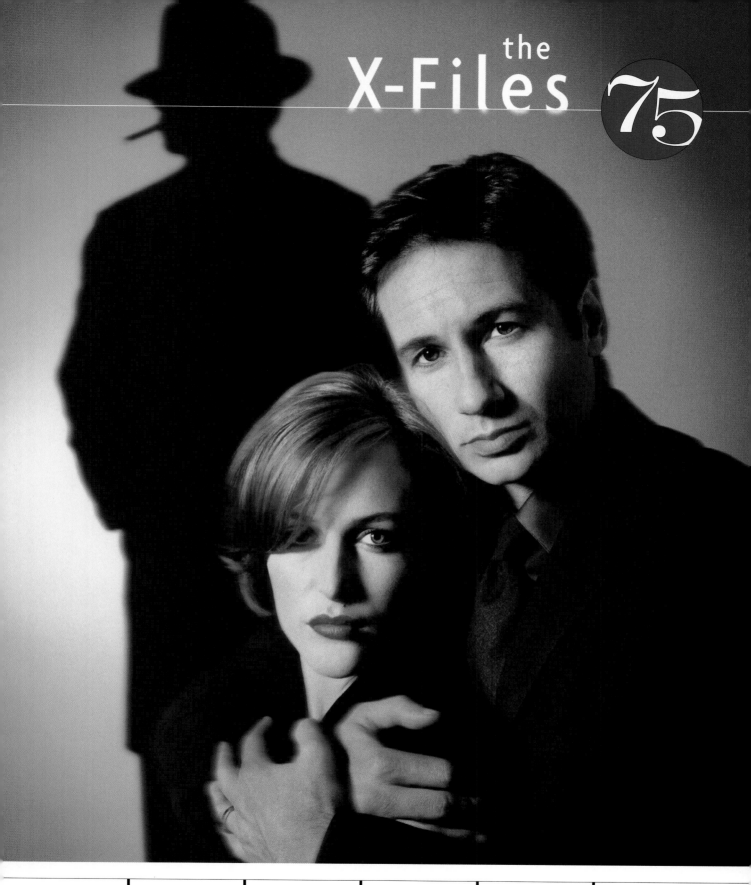

the
X-Files

75

| **SIMPLY THE BEST** | **"BEYOND THE SEA" (JAN 7, 1994)** Anderson and guest villain Brad Dourif are riveting in this Scully/Mulder role-reversal episode. | **"THE ERLENMEYER FLASK" (MAY 13, 1994)** Essential "Mulder and Scully find and lose irrefutable proof of alien life" episode | **"DUANE BARRY/ ASCENSION" (OCT. 14/OCT. 21, 1994)** Scully's abducted in this epic two-parter that adds to the show's mythology. | **"JOSE CHUNG'S 'FROM OUTER SPACE'" (APRIL 12, 1996)** This spooky/silly fable about pomo epistemology is *Rashomon* retold. | **"HOME" (OCT. 11, 1996)** The tragic tale of hillbilly brothers and the dis-membered mother they love too much. Wickedly icky, yet wickedly funny |

Run DMC

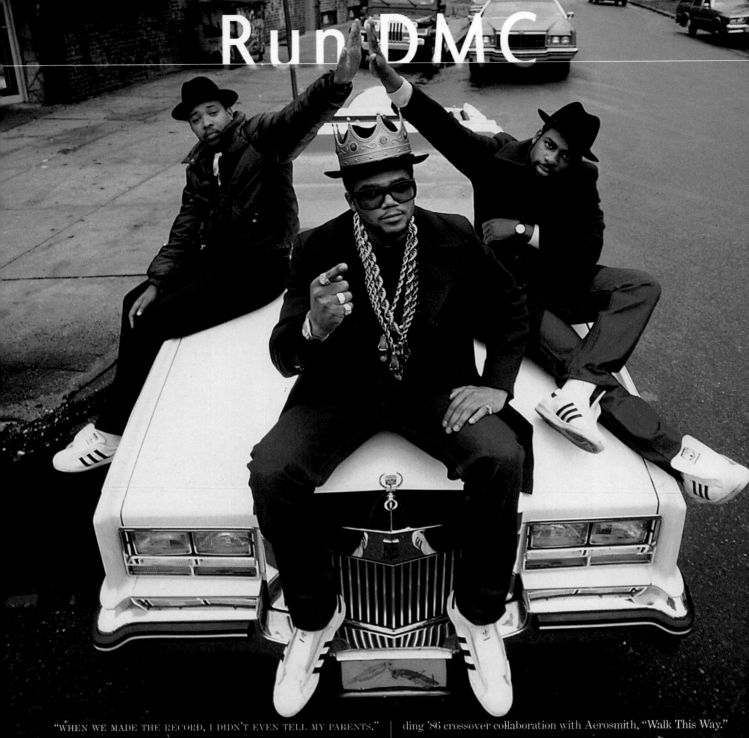

"WHEN WE MADE THE RECORD, I DIDN'T EVEN TELL MY PARENTS," says Darryl McDaniels about "Sucker M.C.'s," Run DMC's debut single, "But then it got so big, I had to take a leave of absence from school—and I've been absent ever since." It was 1983, and McDaniels and buddies Joseph Simmons (Run) and Jason Mizell (Jam Master Jay)—black middle-class college kids from Hollis, Queens—were about to legitimize rap with a string of hugely influential hits, including the genre-shred-

ding '86 crossover collaboration with Aerosmith, "Walk This Way." The latter is something of an understatement: America's youth were soon Adidas-shod duplicates of these hip-hop pioneers. "They are to rap what Hank Williams was to country," says Kid Rock, who, along with fellow latter-day acolyte Fred Durst of Limp Bizkit, appears on Run DMC's upcoming album, *Crown Royal*. "You can't begin to make hip-hop or hip-hop and rock & roll without feeling everything they've done." —TS

76

SIMPLY THE BEST

RUN-D.M.C. (1984)
It stripped music down to little more than voices, beats, and turntable scratches, and laid the blueprint for hip-hop's future.

RAISING HELL (1986)
Many bought it just for "Walk This Way," only to discover they'd purchased the group's most fully realized effort to date.

"MARY, MARY" (1988)
A Monkees cover? Yup—and our boys make it their own without slipping on any banana peels.

SIMPLY THE BEST

LIFE OF BRIAN (1979)
The gospel according to Python skewered all Christian denominations alike, enough to make agnostics of all of us.

Monty Python

77

LOADED UP WITH A QUINTET OF OXBRIDGE WITS AND ONE nomadic Yank animator, disdaining any intention of adhering to formulas or convention, and prepared only to drop the jaws of their frowsty Brit viewers, the comedic speed-blender known as Monty Python began its zany spin 31 years ago on the BBC. The free-form mixture that poured forth—equal parts satire, parody, random violence, naked absurdity, animal abuse, and ribald buffoonery—proved not just piquant but addictive as well, on televisions British and American. The group's films (particularly *Life of Brian* and *Holy Grail*) adhered somewhat more strictly to something resembling narrative, but their joys, too, came in the complete unpredictability of their comic expression—a brand of highbrow silliness later adopted by direct descendant *SNL*. "Sometimes I cannot figure out why we thought something might ever have been funny," says John Cleese, 60, of the Pythons' often inscrutable charm. "And yet, as it happens, I'm laughing at it." —WL

bob Newhart

78

IT SEEMS ODD THAT BOB NEWHART, TV'S SOBEREST STAND-UP comic–turned–sitcom star, is so closely associated with a drinking game. "Hi, Bob!" was spoken 256 times during *The Bob Newhart Show*'s 1972–78 CBS run, and it became the phrase that launched a thousand chugs. "I'd like to be remembered for other things," Newhart, 70, observes. Surely he will, thanks to Newhart's low-key, high-IQ humor and Swiss-watch timing. Still, "Hi, Bob!" isn't such an ill-fitting headline for his legacy. The words seem innocuous, much like Newhart's Chicago shrink (on *The Bob Newhart Show*) and Vermont innkeeper (on CBS' 1982–90 hit *Newhart*), yet they reflect the performer's fundamental approachability. Fans feel like they know him, even if they can't remember from where. "The men all think I was in the service with them," says Newhart. "The women all think I was their first husband." —BF

LIVE AT THE HOLLY-WOOD BOWL (1980)	THE MEANING OF LIFE (1983)	SIMPLY THE BEST	THE BUTTON-DOWN MIND OF BOB NEWHART (1960)	THE BOB NEWHART SHOW (1972–78)	IN & OUT (1997)
Overlooked, but this concert underscores their talent for making just funny material hysterical.	"Every Sperm Is Sacred." Mr. Creosote. Fishy, Fishy. The Grim Reaper. Are you snickering yet?		His debut LP was the first comedy album to hit No. 1 on the *Billboard* charts.	This insanely funny sitcom cast him as a psychologist surrounded by a bunch of charming oddballs.	In the gay–not gay Kevin Kline farce, Newhart—in his first feature film role in years—won raves as a stammering school principal.

79

diana
Ross

▲ *LADY SINGS
THE BLUES* (1972)
In this Billie Holiday
biopic, Ross proved that
not only could she sing
the blues, she could
bring them to vivid life
on the big screen, too.

"LOVE HANGOVER"
(1976)
If there's a cure for
loving the seven
intoxicating minutes
of this record, we
don't want it.

"I'M COMING
OUT" (1980)
This joyful disco-era
whoop amounts to one
of the greatest gay-
pride anthems ever.

"MUSCLES" (1982)
This lush, oddly erotic
song (written by
Michael Jackson)
allowed our Diana to
flex some commercial
muscle yet again.

*THE BEST OF
DIANA ROSS AND
THE SUPREMES*
(1995)
The answer to the
question "Baby, baby,
where did our love go?"
can be found in this
career-spanning compi-
lation, your one-stop
shop for all the dream
girls' smash hits.

MEMO TO HISTORIANS: WHEN THE SHORTLIST OF black women responsible for radical social change is drawn up, be sure Diana Ross' name is near the top. In capturing the hearts of virtually every American male within earshot of a radio—ethnicity be damned—the Supremes' velvet-voiced lead probably did more to improve race relations than a hundred civil rights rallies. (Could any but the most trenchant bigot fail to fall for her demure cooing on "Baby Love"—not to mention the trio's 11 other No. 1 hits?) "Our music wasn't about color," says Ross, 56, and "people didn't listen to us because we were three black girls. They listened because it felt good." Ross, who was nominated for an Academy Award for 1972's *Lady Sings the Blues* and costarred in 1999 with diva-in-training Brandy in ABC's *Double Platinum*, concedes her post-Supremes career as singer and actress has been "up and down." But the woman who showed a generation of singers (from Mary J. Blige to TLC) how it's done is still Taking Care of Business. At one point she was entertaining thoughts of starting her own label and she's currently on the road with the Supremes. Wouldn't you know it? The shy little kid from Detroit's Brewster-Douglass Housing Projects still wants to keep us hangin' on. —TS

SIMPLY THE BEST

AIR JORDAN (1985)

Not the first shoe to be named after a sports star, but certainly the only one—as with the 14 models that have followed—that kids played hooky to get their hands on.

"HANG TIME" (1988)

The Spike Lee-directed Nike spot made Jordan a household name and edged basketball and urban culture toward the mainstream.

"BE LIKE MIKE" (1991)

The tuneful jingle helped solidify Jordan's reputation as a true American hero.

▲ SPACE JAM (1996)

In his first major motion picture, Jordan plays some serious b-ball to help 'toon friends Bugs and Daffy win their freedom from an alien amusement-park owner who wants to make the Looneys a new attraction. Also features NBA stars Larry Bird and Charles Barkley.

MICHAEL JORDAN'S STEAKHOUSE, NEW YORK CITY (1998)

A celebrity restaurant that reflects the owner's impeccable taste, not his fame. Try the porterhouse for two.

YES, HE CHANGED THE GAME OF BASKETBALL with his otherworldly skills. Yes, he forever altered the landscape of sports television, single-handedly turning a second-tier American pastime into a global obsession. But Michael Jordan's deftest crossover move wasn't on the hard court. In 1988, with the help of director Spike Lee, Jordan was featured in a series of groundbreaking Nike commercials that began his transformation from beloved sports hero to totemic media superstar. Says Weiden & Kennedy creative director Jim Riswold, who wrote the ads, "He made us forget about race, appealing to black, white, all colors alike." Just like that, a black athlete was soon selling us—all of us—sports drinks and underwear, phone services and cologne, fast food and shoes. Sure, as a pitchman, Bill Cosby also reached mass audiences. But Jordan brought an electric presence to the role that helped blur the line between art and commerce; one of his spots (a Nike ad) was even turned into a full-length feature (*Space Jam*). Makes you almost forget that the guy used to play a little b-ball. —WL

80

81

agnes
Nixon

EVERY SOCIETY NEEDS A STORYTELLER. THE
Greeks had Aesop. England had Chaucer. Our TV
nation has Agnes Nixon. As creator of *All My
Children*, *One Life to Live*, and *Loving*, she's craft-
ed more than 40 years of compelling serial drama
and reinvented American soap opera. Beginning
under the tutelage of pioneer Irna Phillips, Nixon
soon transformed daytime serials from coffee
klatch melodramas into instruments of social
change—first in 1963 on *The Guiding Light* with a
taboo-breaking uterine cancer plotline, then with
subjects like child abuse, drug addiction, and AIDS.
Nixon also infused the overwrought genre with
much-needed humor (see *Children*'s Susan Lucci
facing down a bear in 1985: "I am Erica Kane, and
you are a filthy beast!"), an element that's as preva-
lent today as issue-based story lines. "I try to
[show viewers], 'There but for the grace of God go
I—or you!'" says Nixon, 72, who still writes *Children*. "Once I started getting letters saying, 'You
saved my life,' I was hooked." So were we. —KB

SIMPLY THE BEST

THE GUIDING LIGHT
(DEBUTED 1952)
Nixon had her first head
writing job on this semi-
nal soap. Her uterine-
cancer-afflicted charac-
ter reportedly helped
spread awareness of the
disease among women.

ONE LIFE TO LIVE
(DEBUTED 1968)
By creating this socially
conscious daytime drama,
Nixon helped break the
genre out of its WASPy
mold by introducing—
gasp!—Jewish and
Catholic families.

▲ ***ALL MY CHILDREN***
(DEBUTED 1970)
Erica Kane lives! Nixon
unleashes the fictional
town of Pine Valley—and
Susan Lucci's mischie-
vous daytime diva—on
the viewing audience.

LOVING
(DEBUTED 1983)
The college town of
Corinth gets Nixon's
sudsy treatment. In 1995,
the show was revamped
into the cool, New York-
based *The City*.

**ACADEMY OF
TELEVISION ARTS
AND SCIENCES HALL
OF FAME** (1993)
After spinning tales for
four decades, Nixon
becomes the first female
writer to be inducted
into the TV Hall of Fame.

eric Clapton

82

OVER THE YEARS, ERIC CLAPTON HAS BEEN many things: Psychedelic dilettante. Flashy improviser. Tormented lover. Stone junkie. Grieving father. Recovering addict. But his most enduring persona remains that of the lifelong bluesman who uses pain as fodder for his art. Even when they're not by-the-numbers blues, many of his songs—"Layla," "Promises," "Tears in Heaven"—still reek of ineffable sadness. Like his venerated hero, Robert Johnson, the reclusive guitarist has always seemed a conduit for his hurt-filled music—and an enigma as an individual. "Blues is his total base of everything," says John Mayall, in whose band, the Blues Breakers, Clapton first gained notoriety as the premier white axman of the '60s. "Beyond that, he's a very private person. He doesn't put himself out there very much." Indeed, Clapton's recent bankrolling of Crossroads Centre, a drug and alcohol treatment facility in the Bahamas, tells us more about who he really is than most of his interviews. Yet amazingly for a grizzled '60s veteran, he remains a vital force on the modern pop scene, and his influence can clearly be heard in the playing of young guitarists like Jonny Lang and Kenny Wayne Shepherd. "I think that the ultimate guitar hero should be a dispenser of wisdom," Clapton, 55, has said. "That should come through in the playing." Perhaps wisely, old Slowhand continues to let his music do the talking. —TS

john
Grisham

IT'S NOT OFTEN A RUMPLED MISSISSIPPI writer can intimidate a flashy Hollywood director, but that's just the effect John Grisham had on Joel Schumacher. "Test audiences loved it," Schumacher recalls of his '96 feature version of *A Time to Kill.* "But if John didn't like it, that would have been a big blow." A lowly scribe causing tectonic shifts in Tinseltown? Consider the evidence: his novels have spawned films grossing more than $522 million combined; in '93, rights to *The Chamber* were bought for a phenomenal $3.75 million—based on a *synopsis*; three years later, *The Runaway Jury* was sold for more than $8 million. Legal thrillers existed before Grisham, now 45, but it took his frenetically paced and morally centered narratives to change publishing. Says *Time* star Matthew McConaughey: "It's obvious he cares about mankind." —CLARISSA CRUZ

PHOTOGRAPH BY PORTER GIFFORD

PHOTOGRAPH BY NIGEL PARRY

SIMPLY THE BEST

A TIME TO KILL (1989)
His inflammatory debut came and went without so much as a publishing peep, but the Southern-fried tale of a young attorney defending a father who murders his daughter's rapists is Grisham at his most heartfelt.

THE FIRM (1991)
Grisham's second novel—about an ambitious yuppie lawyer seduced by a slick Tennessee firm—introduced the tax attorney-turned-author to the world in crackling, twisty-plotted style.

THE CHAMBER (1994)
Hot on the heels of the box office success of the film adaptations of *The Firm* and *The Pelican Brief,* Hollywood paid a then-record $3.75 million for the rights to this death-row thriller—before even seeing a first draft.

THE OXFORD AMERICAN (1996)
In the pages of his Mississippi-based literary magazine, Grisham becomes a spokesperson in the culture wars, blasting Oliver Stone and his film *Natural Born Killers* for inspiring copycat killings.

THE TESTAMENT (1999)
Eschewing his usual courtroom environs for the mosquitoey, reptile-heavy Brazilian rain forest (and painting his most conflicted hero yet), Grisham revitalizes his best-selling legal formula with a stunning change of scenery.

84

SUPPOSE SOME OTHER ACTOR—SAY, DAVID NIVEN (the writer's first choice)—had been cast as the original big-screen Bond in '62. Where would Sean Connery be today? Right here in these pages. Because while he may have begun with Her Majesty's Secret Service, his career certainly didn't end there. Over the past 40 years—in brainy action pics like *The Man Who Would Be King* and *The Untouchables* (Connery's only Oscar-winning turn)—the no-bull star has proven himself every bit as indestructible as the martini-sipping 007. "I've never tried to play younger," the Scotsman, now 69, explains of his longevity. "I've always played older. And my hair disappearing early made the transition a lot easier." Don't underestimate the lack of vanity: The secret of his eternal sexiness may be that—unlike so many others—he never cared that his hair disappeared. —B S

sean
Connery

WHEN VAUDEVILLIAN VARIETY SHOWS WERE BEING DRIVEN OFF INTO THE CATHODE-RAY sunset, Carol Burnett took the format for one last, loopy spin. A daffy, unpredictable talent who could sing, dance, act, and deliver a mean Tarzan yell, she turned *The Carol Burnett Show* (1967–78) into one of TV's longest-running musical-comedy series while breaking down a few walls—including the fourth. (Was the whole chatting-with-the-audience thing a precursor to Oprah?) No one since has matched the versatility of Burnett, who, with a tug of an ear, acutely tweaked hundreds of archetypes from cleaning ladies to starlets. "Lots of people work from the inside out, but I worked from the outside in," Burnett, 67, says. "I wasn't afraid to look awful. Sometimes we'd have a sketch that wasn't good, but you put a wig on, boobs hanging down to your navel, and suddenly…" Magic. —DS

85

carol **Burnett**

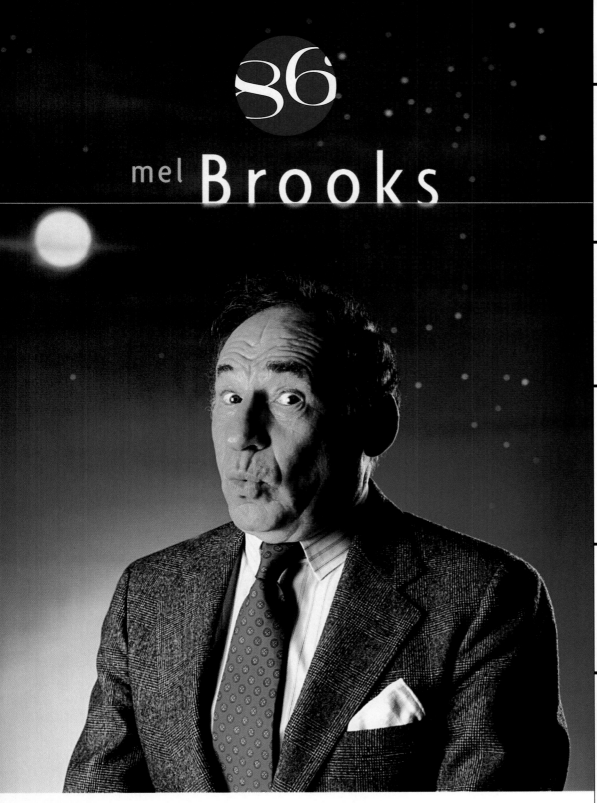

86
mel Brooks

SIMPLY
THE BEST

YOUR SHOW OF SHOWS (1950–54)
It's one thing to be a stand-out writer on a TV comedy show. It's another when your coworkers include Neil Simon, Woody Allen, and Carl Reiner.

THE 2,000-YEAR-OLD MAN (1961)
By giving voice to the two-millennia man on the hugely popular album, Brooks assured himself a following as a performer.

THE PRODUCERS (1968)
The story of two men trying to craft a guaranteed musical flop titled *Springtime for Hilter* reached singular depths of deliriously bad taste...

BLAZING SADDLES (1974)
...at least until this raunchy Western about a black sheriff keeping the peace in the racist town of Rock Ridge.

▲ **YOUNG FRANKENSTEIN (1974)**
The parody is so powerfully goofy that it is impossible to watch the James Whale masterpiece *Bride of Frankenstein* without distraction.

BUT SERIOUSLY, FOLKS, THE ESSENCE OF A Mel Brooks joke—in *The Producers*, in *Blazing Saddles*, in the *2,000-Year-Old Man* sketch—is its navigation of burlesquely broad material through the straits of exact wit. "I happened to see [Brooks' *Young Frankenstein*] last night," says Teri Garr, who played the buxom lab assistant Inga in that 1974 parody. "Mel combines that sort of eighth-grade adolescent humor and an old-fashioned borscht-belt sensibility." Indeed, as a veteran of Catskills resort stand-up and Sid Caesar's seminal *Your Show of Shows*, Brooks, 74, is the link between historic shtick and later strains of deft daffiness, including the rapid-fire gag work of *Airplane!* and the acute lampoons of *The Simpsons*. On set, Garr says, "he insists that everyone be laughing all the time." On screen, at his best, no insistence is necessary. —TP

87
steven
Bochco

YOU CAN THANK BRUCE DERN FOR STEVEN Bochco's TV career. In 1971, an out-of-work Bochco accepted a $750-a-week gig rewriting the sci-fi flick *Silent Running*. "I watched Dern screw up that script so obscenely by turning it into a hippie-dippy tract," he recalls. "I got such a sense of the powerlessness of movie writers that I became a TV producer to protect my own stuff." After cutting his teeth on conventional cop shows like *Columbo*, he proceeded to undo everything done before with NBC's *Hill Street Blues*. Bochco proceeded to give Perry Mason a glittery wake-up call with NBC's *L.A. Law*, then re-reinvented the cop show with ABC's *NYPD Blue*. Now 56, he's giving TV docs a face-lift with CBS' African-American hospital drama *City of Angels*. Clearly, this man never heeded the advice of *Hill Street*'s Sgt. Phil Esterhaus: "Let's be careful out there." —BF

BALONEY. THAT'S THE SECRET TO LORETTA LYNN'S SUCCESS. In 1960, when the aspiring singer and her husband, Mooney, were peddling her first single to radio stations, the couple slept in their car and subsisted on baloney sandwiches. Their mettle paid off with "I'm a Honky Tonk Girl," Lynn's first of some 69 hits, most of them self-penned paeans to hang-tough women that introduced Americans to a country music rarely heard beyond hardscrabble mountain towns like Butcher Hollow, Ky., where she grew up. The sound was *real*. "When you listen to her sing, you feel like you've just had a conversation with her," says acolyte Lee Ann Womack. "That's what makes her one of the greats."

In 1980, Hollywood turned the singer's best-selling autobiography, *Coal Miner's Daughter*, into a box office hit, yet the 65-year-old Lynn continues to cling to her backwoods roots. Says Randy Scruggs, producer of her upcoming album, "Whenever she had a really great day [recording], she ordered in baloney for everybody." —ALANNA NASH

loretta
Lynn

88

SIMPLY THE BEST	HILL STREET BLUES (1981–87)	L.A. LAW (1986–94)	COP ROCK (1990)	NYPD BLUE (1993–)	MURDER ONE (1995–97)
	There were TV dramas before it. And there were TV dramas after it—but they were never the same.	The undeniably appealing attorneys of McKenzie, Brackman inspired a million law-school applications.	The series lasted only three months, but people still remember its singing detectives 10 years later.	When Dennis Franz and Co. dropped trou, they simultaneously raised the bar for excellence in prime time.	For viewers with long attention spans, this legal serial proved more captivating than Court TV.

SIMPLY THE BEST

DECCA RECORDS (1962)
Producer Owen Bradley takes a chance on a feisty newcomer whose songs paint her as she is.

GRAND OLE OPRY (1962)
The Opry leads to work with the Wilburn Brothers and duets with Ernest Tubb and Conway Twitty.

"COAL MINER'S DAUGHTER" (1970)
Her self-penned theme song spawns a best-selling memoir and a hit film starring Sissy Spacek.

HONKY TONK GIRL: THE LORETTA LYNN COLLECTION (1994)
The best primer, with an overview of the songs that shaped her persona

20TH CENTURY MASTERS: THE MILLENNIUM...CONWAY TWITTY & LORETTA LYNN (2000)
Her best duets with Twitty

WOMEN WHO SANG THE BLUES, FEMALE POP STARS, AND PLENTY of folkies came before her. But until Janis Joplin crashed the San Francisco music scene in 1963, there weren't any women who rocked. "It was mind-blowing to watch her," says John Byrne Cooke, Joplin's road manager. "[It was as if] she could sing more than one note, she could sing *chords*." In 1970, months before dying at age 27 of a heroin overdose, Joplin was working on *Pearl*, which would become her most notable album ("Me and Bobby McGee," "Cry Baby"). But it was her soulbaring live shows that captured her essence—like lightning in a bottle. "Janis lived through the other 23 hours of the day for that one hour on stage. She came off and she was exhausted, sweaty, disheveled. But that was what made her Janis," says Cooke. "She didn't give much thought to blazing a trail for women. She just went ahead and did what she did. Which, of course, is the best way to start a revolution." —JS

SIMPLY THE BEST

MONTEREY POP (1967)
Her sultry rendition of "Ball and Chain" at this monumental festival insta-launched the hippie chick.

LIVE AT WINTER-LAND '68 (1998)
Janis brought down the house with "Down on Me" and "Summertime."

CHEAP THRILLS (1968)
Showcases Joplin's raw and emotional vocal range on future classic "Piece of My Heart"

I GOT DEM OL' KOZMIC BLUES AGAIN MAMA! (1969)
Joplin's first solo venture features classic tunes "Little Girl Blue" and "Try."

PEARL (1971)
This seminal rock album includes the heart-wrenching "Cry Baby" and the oft-covered "Me and Bobby McGee."

PHOTOGRAPH BY ELLIOTT MOSS LANDY

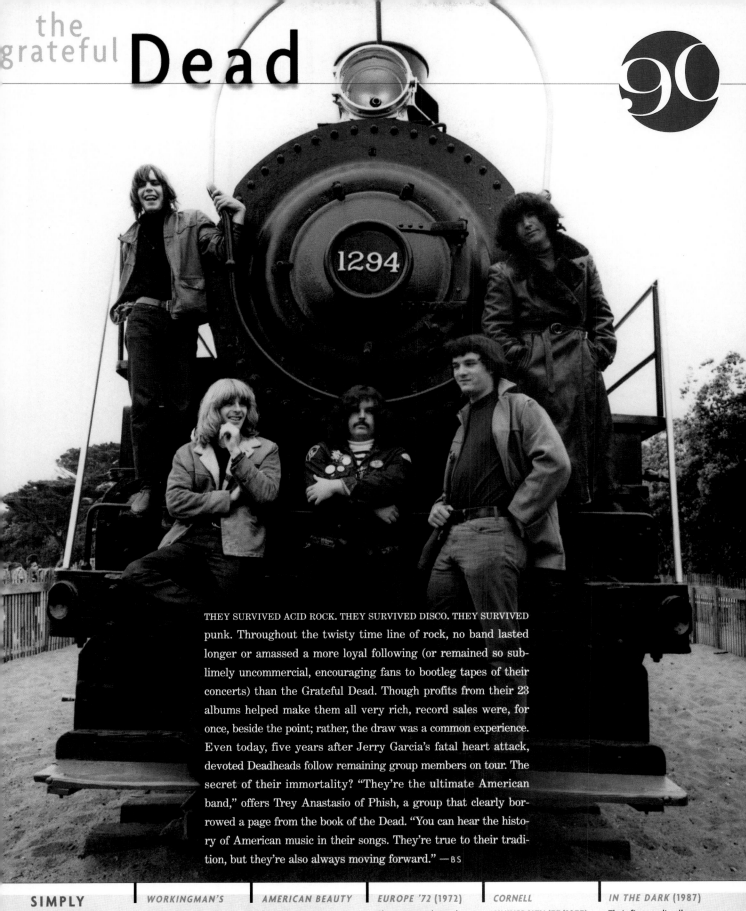

the grateful Dead

1294

THEY SURVIVED ACID ROCK. THEY SURVIVED DISCO. THEY SURVIVED punk. Throughout the twisty time line of rock, no band lasted longer or amassed a more loyal following (or remained so sublimely uncommercial, encouraging fans to bootleg tapes of their concerts) than the Grateful Dead. Though profits from their 23 albums helped make them all very rich, record sales were, for once, beside the point; rather, the draw was a common experience. Even today, five years after Jerry Garcia's fatal heart attack, devoted Deadheads follow remaining group members on tour. The secret of their immortality? "They're the ultimate American band," offers Trey Anastasio of Phish, a group that clearly borrowed a page from the book of the Dead. "You can hear the history of American music in their songs. They're true to their tradition, but they're also always moving forward." —BS

SIMPLY THE BEST

WORKINGMAN'S DEAD (1970)
As a stripped-down blues-folk band, the Dead crank out their first masterpiece, fueled by "Casey Jones."

AMERICAN BEAUTY (1970)
Their finest moment in the studio, with "Truckin'," "Sugar Magnolia," and "Box of Rain"

EUROPE '72 (1972)
Three trippy platters' worth of vinyl noodling and trance-dance space jams. The best live album for the law-abiding.

CORNELL UNIVERSITY '77 (1977)
Universally regarded by the tie-dyed cognoscenti as the Dead's primo concert bootleg.

IN THE DARK (1987)
Their first studio album in seven years gave the psychedelic grand-daddies the out-of-the-blue hit "Touch of Grey."

robin
Williams

SIMPLY THE BEST

MORK & MINDY (1978–82)
Spinning off from the series *Happy Days*, the sitcom about a sweet nutcase from the planet Ork showcased Williams in all his frenzied madness.

GOOD MORNING, VIETNAM (1987)
Williams' dramatic turn as Armed Forces DJ Adrian Cronauer finally proved to audiences that he could carry a film. His monologues were the highlight.

▲ ALADDIN (1992)
You never actually see him, but Williams' embodiment of the cartoon genie was the perfect fit for his one-and-only brand of schizoid humor.

MRS. DOUBTFIRE (1993)
Tons of latex, a hideous dress, and a high-pitched voice equaled Williams' most out-there physical stretch—and his biggest commercial success to date.

GOOD WILL HUNTING (1997)
Returning to second-tier status, Williams revealed hidden depth as a schlumpfy shrink and scored his first Oscar.

HE'S BEEN CALLED A HUMAN CARTOON, AND WITH his antic, everything-but-the-kitchen-sink performance style, Robin Williams can seem more Looney Tunes than Method. But the description hardly does him justice. Ever since ABC's *Mork & Mindy* (1978–82), Williams, 48, has created uniquely layered characters, equal parts yuk and soul, in films like *Good Morning, Vietnam* and *Mrs. Doubtfire*. Those surprised by his somber, Oscar-winning turn in *Good Will Hunting* need only remember he was a student of a very serious acting school (Juilliard). Still, his signature is his comic vitality, so much so that he can spend an entire film (the 1999 robot comedy *Bicentennial Man*) hidden in a suit of armor. Says director Chris Columbus, "The moment we saw the first dailies, we knew: There was no doubt who was inside that suit." —DK

91

PHOTOGRAPH BY GWENDOLEN CATES

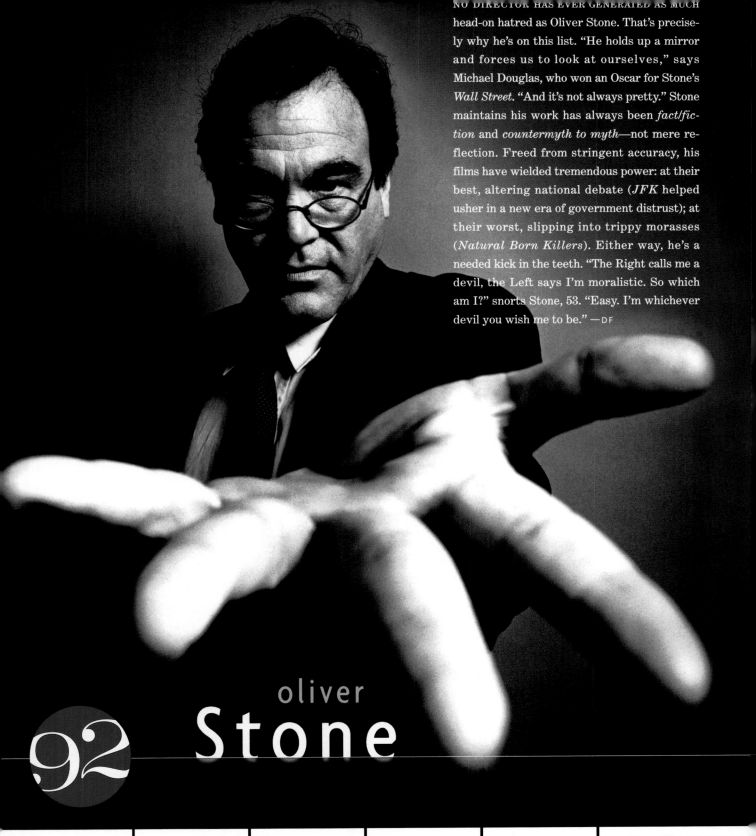

NO DIRECTOR HAS EVER GENERATED AS MUCH head-on hatred as Oliver Stone. That's precisely why he's on this list. "He holds up a mirror and forces us to look at ourselves," says Michael Douglas, who won an Oscar for Stone's *Wall Street*. "And it's not always pretty." Stone maintains his work has always been *fact/fiction* and *countermyth to myth*—not mere reflection. Freed from stringent accuracy, his films have wielded tremendous power: at their best, altering national debate (*JFK* helped usher in a new era of government distrust); at their worst, slipping into trippy morasses (*Natural Born Killers*). Either way, he's a needed kick in the teeth. "The Right calls me a devil, the Left says I'm moralistic. So which am I?" snorts Stone, 53. "Easy. I'm whichever devil you wish me to be." —DF

oliver
Stone

92

SIMPLY THE BEST

PLATOON (1986)
Among the most celebrated—and still the most poignant—examinations of Vietnam and its corrosive effects

WALL STREET (1987)
One of those movies that so purely captured its era ("Greed is good") that it became an instant classic

JFK (1991)
It spurred a debate over the nature of history and prefigured a mistrust of government seen everywhere from Waco to *The X-Files*.

NATURAL BORN KILLERS (1994)
The fact that it's still the subject of litigation and debate underscores how raw a nerve it hit.

NIXON (1995)
The embodiment of the twin hallmarks of his work: historical monkey-wrenching and a spellbinding hallucinogenic style

bob
Fosse

BEFORE HIM, MOVIE CHOREOGRAPHY CAME IN THREE BASIC flavors: kaleidoscopic (à la Busby Berkeley), elegant (Fred Astaire), or athletic (Gene Kelly). Then Fosse revolutionized dancing the way Elvis changed pop: He sexed it up. "His vision was so strong as a choreographer, it overshadowed everything else," says Janet Leigh, star of Fosse's first big film, 1955's *My Sister Eileen.* Perhaps, but what a lot of else there was. Honing his directing chops on '60s theatrical hits, Fosse achieved full-blown auteurship with 1972's *Cabaret,* stealing the Best Director Oscar from *The Godfather*'s Francis Ford Coppola. The following year, he won an Emmy for a Liza Minnelli TV special, plus a Tony for *Pippin.* On through *Lenny,* the semiautobiographical *All That Jazz,* and the scabrous showbiz exposé *Star 80,* Fosse (who died in 1987 at 60 of the heart failure *Jazz* predicted) razzle-dazzled us as much with editing, lighting, and cinematography as with his decadent dance steps—an Orson Welles in tap shoes and tails. —SD

elvis
Costello

94

PIGEON-TOED AND PISSED OFF, ELVIS COSTELLO announced himself as rock's most passionate singer upon arrival: Bob Dylan reincarnated as a virtuosic, pun-spewing punk, angry at the radio, the world, and, most of all, his model girlfriend. That was 1977; 23 years later, he's less the thoughtful rageaholic and more the graceful balladeer, at least to a generation more familiar with his Burt Bacharach collaborations, his *Austin Powers* cameo, and his *Notting Hill*-generated hit, the Charles Aznavour cover "She." There are drawbacks, of course, to virtuosity. "I would've expected more criticism for trying to peddle the same record 15 times," says Costello, 45, of fans who preferred his earlier, crankier work to diversions into country and classical. "But it's only if you want people to love you all the time that you should worry about these things." Some things, thankfully, never change. —CW

| **SIMPLY THE BEST** | *MY SISTER EILEEN* (1955) Showing off Fosse's hip-swiveling sensibility, it's one of his more appealing turns in front of a movie camera. | *THE PAJAMA GAME* (1957) Fosse's bowler-hat choreography in the number "Steam Heat" is so elegantly sexy it looks like it was just filmed. | *SWEET CHARITY* (1969) Full of leggy acrobatics that put those Gap ads to shame. Just skip the saccharine number "I'm a Brass Band." | **SIMPLY THE BEST** | *THIS YEAR'S MODEL* (1978) The breakup album of all breakup albums: furious, self-righteous, explosively clever. |

95

HE LOVES SCENARIOS ABOUT HIGH-TECH MONOLITHS LAID LOW by glitches: a killer robot KO'd by a scrappy woman in both *Terminator* films, a terraforming colony overrun by aliens, the unsinkable *Titanic* sunk by a puncture. And in making ever-grander spectacles of destruction, James Cameron, 45, has flirted with disaster himself, burning up budgets (at $200 million plus, *Titanic* is the all-time cost champ as well as the world box office king) and driving his crews mercilessly (the *Terminator 2: Judgment Day* team had T-shirts reading "*Terminator 3: Not With Me!*"). But as weight lifters say, no pain, no gain. "He gets so passionate, he's like a little boy," says Arnold Schwarzenegger of the man who made him a megastar in *T1*. And it's through such no-brakes intensity that Cameron achieves unconditional veracity; you are on that ship, that planet, that plane. Of all the auteurs who are fond of treating studios like expensive Erector sets, he's built the coolest toys. —SD

james
Cameron

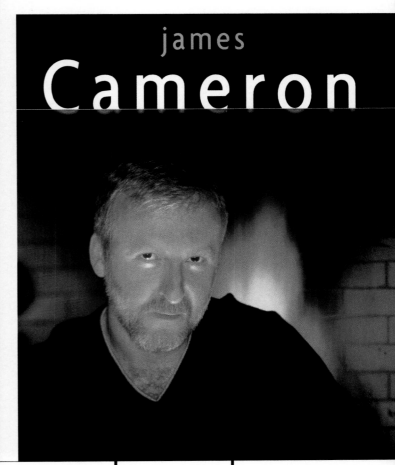

SIMPLY THE BEST

CAMERON PHOTOGRAPH BY GREGORY HEISLER

diane Keaton

"WELL, HOW DID YOU MAKE THIS MISTAKE?" DIANE KEATON WANTS to know, upon learning she's one of EW's greatest. "Who are the crazy people who put this together?" It's the sort of charmingly neurotic answer that got Keaton elected in the first place. More than any other actress, Keaton shone by being familiar. Whether playing lovable shiksas in Woody Allen films or *The Godfather*'s WASP Everywoman, she grounded her roles in the recognizable anxieties of everyday life. She's evolved from single girl (*Looking for Mr. Goodbar*) to working mother (*Baby Boom*) to gay divorcée (*The First Wives Club*), yet somehow she always remained the closest thing the movies have to us. Not that that has made her more self-assured. "I'm sure if you did this two weeks from now," she says, "I'd be off the list." We think not. —DH

96

SIMPLY THE BEST

THE GODFATHER (1972)
As Kay Adams, she added a dose of humanity and emotion to the under-world of organized crime.

ANNIE HALL (1977)
Playing the kook opposite Woody Allen's neurotic earned her an Oscar and made ties and floppy hats must-have accessories.

THE FIRST WIVES CLUB (1996)
Meet the new housewife: affluent, fed up, and out for vengeance on ex-hus-bands with "trophy wives."

SIMPLY THE BEST

MAVERICK (1957–62)
Forget about Mel Gibson—Garner is, was, and always will be the roguishly charming Bret Maverick.

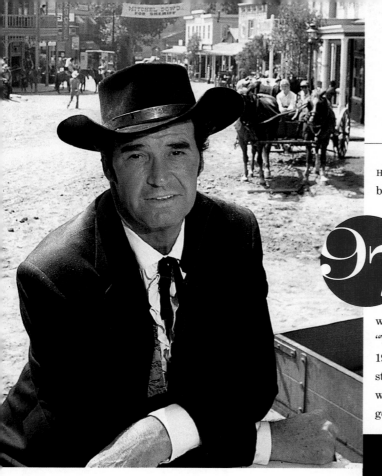

james Garner

.97

HE WAS NOMINATED FOR AN OSCAR (*MURPHY'S ROMANCE*), AND breezed through scores of popular films (*The Great Escape, The Americanization of Emily*), but somehow his pulchritude never translated into major-movie stardom. It was the new medium of TV that allowed Garner to flourish, chiefly through the subversion of his good looks. A bummed-out Don Juan, he imbued roguish 19th-century gambler Bret Maverick and down-at-the-heels '70s gumshoe Jim Rockford with a then-rare blend of twinkle-eyed charm and cynicism. "They're antiheroes," says Garner, who debuted on *Cheyenne* in 1955. "When *Maverick* went on, there were only Westerns with steely-eyed sheriffs, and he didn't want to fight. When *Rockford* went on, there were all these brave detectives, and he knew you'd get hurt being brave." The birth of loser chic. —BF

garth Brooks

.98

IN JUNE 1989, A SOFT-SPOKEN SINGER, NEWLY SIGNED TO CAPITOL Records, took the stage at a Kansas City theater, tipped his Stetson to the crowd of 334, and launched into his first hit, "Much Too Young (to Feel This Damn Old)." Promoter Tuffy Williams remembers, "He was so scared the crowd wouldn't like him, he didn't move two steps from the mic all night." It was the last time Garth Brooks, now 38, ever stood still. Within two years, he'd raised country from the dead, luring fans into a national line dance and inspiring the pop-infused likes of Shania Twain. He'd go on to sell 90 million records, within shouting distance of the Beatles as best-selling artist of all time. But his real gift is his exuberant showmanship, more Kiss than kiss-the-cheatin'-wife-goodbye. Says Williams: "On stage, he's some kind of crazy man. I don't know who enjoys it more, the fans or him." —SM

THE ROCKFORD FILES (1974–80)	MURPHY'S ROMANCE (1985)	SIMPLY THE BEST	GARTH BROOKS (1989)	ROPIN' THE WIND (1991)	DOUBLE LIVE (1998)
L.A. PI Jim Rockford's fee was $200 a day plus expenses, but Garner's sly performance was priceless.	He earned a well-deserved Oscar nod—even though the easygoing Garner never seems to be *acting*.		His debut spins off four top 10 country singles, including "If Tomorrow Never Comes" and "The Dance."	Crossover *ka-ching!* The first album ever to debut at No. 1 on *Billboard*'s pop *and* country album charts.	It set a record for first-week sales with 1.08 million copies, beating previous champs Pearl Jam, whose *Vs.* sold 950,000 units.

spike
Lee

99

AT ONCE AN ADMAN AND A REVOLUTION-ary, a deft self-promoter and an ideologue of real conviction, Spike Lee, 43, makes stylish entertainments, and he makes them morally urgent. His first post–film-school feature, the frisky, funny _She's Gotta Have It_ (1986), thrust him into the role of The Black Director and assured his status as a figurehead. "He gave you the feeling that anyone could [make movies]," says M. Night Shyamalan, the Indian-American director of _The Sixth Sense_. "He made me start thinking that I could do it as a career." The controversies that greeted _Do the Right Thing_, his tabloid alarum, and _Malcolm X_, his meditative epic, prove the importance of Lee's voice: At the studio level, none of his peers can match his commitment to making serious films about race and class and power. As such, he cannot be said to have any peers at all. —TP

THE PRETENDERS' SELF-TITLED FIRST ALBUM remains, arguably, the greatest debut in rock history. That this classic was conceived by a woman might not be as shocking to a Lilith-sated Generation Y, but when Chrissie Hynde broke out of the new-wave pack in early 1980, the effect opened rock up for the disenfranchised 51 percent. "I don't feel I'm a pioneer," says Hynde, 48. "I've heard other women say they had to work harder because they were a girl. But this is show business, and if you're the odd one out, that's called a gimmick and works in your favor." If Hynde was a novelty, it was in her ability to write pungently about lust without selling sex, to appear both tough and tender without fulfilling anyone's bitch or simp stereotypes. Many a Courtney Love has tried, but it's a near-impossible act to follow. "There's not many female rockers," figures Hynde, "so although I'm tempted to try other things, I like to deliver what we set out to do. And I don't find many bands to outrock us, once we get going." —CW

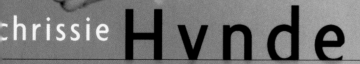

chrissie Hynde

SIMPLY THE BEST	*PRETENDERS* (1980)	*PRETENDERS II* (1981)	*LEARNING TO CRAWL* (1984)	"DON'T GET ME WRONG" (1986)	"NIGHT IN MY VEINS" (1994)
	The *Citizen Kane* of rock albums? Well, Hynde did manage the most fully formed debut since Orson Welles tried directing.	Underrated when it was released, *II* now pales only against its predecessor. With "The Adultress" and "Talk of the Town."	The first, most convincingly tough-minded, and still greatest female rocker is a model proud mom, too.	Boy meets girl, Motown bass line meets girl-group exultation, and leather meets bubblegum.	It's just her imagination running away, but you can feel the sweat in this lust-packed pop daydream.

the
Sweet Hereafter

After all this fond reminiscing about the most eminent celebrities of our era, it's time to consider the future of showbiz. Who will be the best and the brightest of the next 100 years? Here, a brief look at 10 talented young guns who stand to rise to the ranks of Greatest Entertainer. —BY SCOTT BROWN

First she was Brad Pitt's girlfriend. Then she was Ben Affleck's girlfriend. And for a while, that's all the shutterbugs cared about. But after running the flashbulb gauntlet (something she still does exceptionally well), Paltrow, 28, was back at work, steadily building her reputation as a versatile leading lady—not to mention one hell of a clotheshorse (Calvin Klein should pay her royalties). Then came her Oscar-winning turn as a luminous courtier–turned–cross-dressing thespian in *Shakespeare in Love*, and suddenly Paltrow was being celebrated as the next Grace Kelly. "I generally like where I am right now because I feel like I'm on a good path," she once told EW. That's putting it mildly. Just ask the next lucky guy who gets to be Gwyneth Paltrow's boyfriend.

Gwyneth Paltrow

Ben Stiller

When you're best known as "that guy whose thingie got caught in his zipper" in *There's Something About Mary*, getting respect as an actor-writer-director promises to be an uphill battle. At least, that's what conventional wisdom says. But there's very little that's conventional about Ben Stiller, the 34-year-old comic wunderkind who first appeared on the scene in the early '90s with such dead-on, zeitgeist-tapping experiments as *Reality Bites*—widely acknowledged as the seminal Gen-X movie—and the short-lived but warmly remembered *Ben Stiller Show*, wherein the chameleonic host explored such topical matters as Yakov Smirnoff's post-Soviet act (he's been reduced to kvetching about China) with the sort of anarchic irony that would become the hallmark of the age. Eight years later, Stiller hasn't lost his touch. His work in *Flirting With Disaster* and *Mary* presented us with a sleeker nebbish for the new millennium—and a possible successor to Woody Allen. Which is fine, as long as he doesn't start adopting children with Janeane Garofalo.

Will Smith

"You're not afraid of me," Will Smith once told a crowd of reporters. "I'm fun for everybody." Spoken like a true crossover phenomenon. The erstwhile Fresh Prince has delighted Americans, black and white, for over 10 years, which raises the question: Is the $20 million alien slayer who ushered in his own personal *Willennium* last fall the same charming doofus who sang about how "parents just don't understand" in the late '80s? You betcha. Smith, 31, knew then what he knows now—that menace might be fashionable, but it's not consistently bankable. He just happened to be several years and two tremendous July 4 weekend openings (*Independence Day* and *Men in Black*) away from realizing his full potential. Ironically, his galactic success has become his biggest liability (consider the dashed expectations for *Wild Wild West*), which is probably why his next summer film (*The Legend of Bagger Vance*) was directed by Robert Redford. With typical savvy, Smith is balancing prestige and profitability—a strategy that promises to keep him fresh well into the next Willennium.

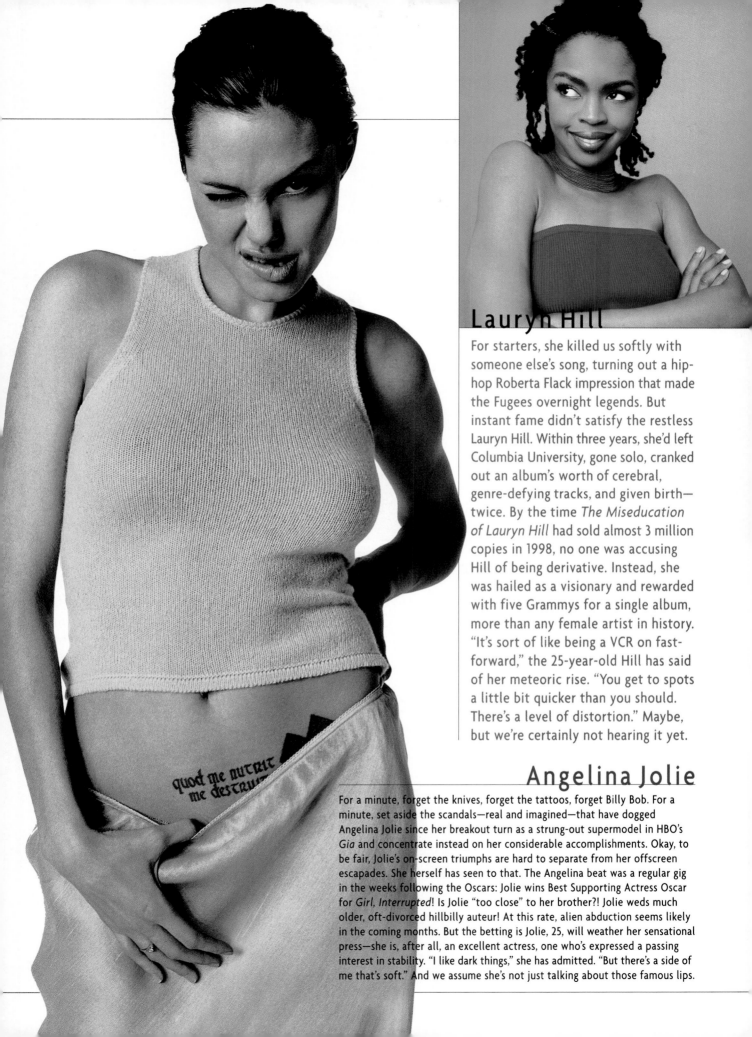

Lauryn Hill

For starters, she killed us softly with someone else's song, turning out a hip-hop Roberta Flack impression that made the Fugees overnight legends. But instant fame didn't satisfy the restless Lauryn Hill. Within three years, she'd left Columbia University, gone solo, cranked out an album's worth of cerebral, genre-defying tracks, and given birth—twice. By the time *The Miseducation of Lauryn Hill* had sold almost 3 million copies in 1998, no one was accusing Hill of being derivative. Instead, she was hailed as a visionary and rewarded with five Grammys for a single album, more than any female artist in history. "It's sort of like being a VCR on fast-forward," the 25-year-old Hill has said of her meteoric rise. "You get to spots a little bit quicker than you should. There's a level of distortion." Maybe, but we're certainly not hearing it yet.

Angelina Jolie

For a minute, forget the knives, forget the tattoos, forget Billy Bob. For a minute, set aside the scandals—real and imagined—that have dogged Angelina Jolie since her breakout turn as a strung-out supermodel in HBO's *Gia* and concentrate instead on her considerable accomplishments. Okay, to be fair, Jolie's on-screen triumphs are hard to separate from her offscreen escapades. She herself has seen to that. The Angelina beat was a regular gig in the weeks following the Oscars: Jolie wins Best Supporting Actress Oscar for *Girl, Interrupted*! Is Jolie "too close" to her brother?! Jolie weds much older, oft-divorced hillbilly auteur! At this rate, alien abduction seems likely in the coming months. But the betting is Jolie, 25, will weather her sensational press—she is, after all, an excellent actress, one who's expressed a passing interest in stability. "I like dark things," she has admitted. "But there's a side of me that's soft." And we assume she's not just talking about those famous lips.

Chris Rock

"There is a glut of a certain kind of black comedian and a certain kind of white comedian," Chris Rock once remarked, with typically brutal candor. "Stand-up sucks right now." That may be true, but Rock, 35, isn't part of the problem. He's also not immediately classifiable as "a certain kind of comedian." Sure, he riffs on the black experience, but you're out of luck if you think your skin color will protect you from his sulfuric critiques. Rock is the anti–Will Smith: He crossed over by trashing everybody. And he's not sorry. Why should he be? His late-night talk show is going strong, his HBO stand-up specials have reinvigorated the genre, and his first star vehicle—a remake of *Heaven Can Wait* called *I Was Made to Love Her*—opens in the fall. "The only thing I can do wrong is not be funny," said Rock. If that's the case, then he's doing everything right.

Lisa Kudrow

We're always pleasantly surprised when an actor's real-life behavior exceeds her TV character's limitations. So naturally, we were overjoyed to see Lisa Kudrow, 36, playing hard-nosed union boss to her fellow Friends as they bargained for higher salaries this spring. Flaky Phoebe—a tough negotiator? "I worry about the future," Kudrow once said, but of all her costars, she probably has the least to worry about. Dealt *Friends'* most pigeonholeable role, she transformed a one-note airhead into a complicated woman struggling with maternal instincts, artistic ambitions, and, yes, chronic ditsiness. "Phoebe is not dumb," Kudrow famously proclaimed. "She's a nitwit, but she's not dumb." (She once took Matt Lauer to the mat for using the D-word to describe Ms. Buffay.) Having made her point, she turned to drama, turning herself into the bitter, middle-aged Lucia in 1998's *The Opposite of Sex*, and washed away every trace of her celebrated bubble-headedness. Once again, she surprised us. It's safe to say she'll be surprising us for years to come.

Dixie Chicks

Their name and image would seem to land them just shy of outright cutesiness: a trio of dye-job cowgirls singing sweet little ditties about…spousal murder and "mattress dancin'"? See, that's the problem with selling short the Dixie Chicks (above, from left, Martie Seidel, 30, Natalie Maines, 25, and Emily Robison, 27). Just when you're ready to consign their breakout, crossover, Grammy-winning album *Wide Open Spaces* to the fad-and-fluke bin, they follow up with the top-selling *Fly*, which embraces gritty themes while preserving their traditional country instrumentation, a real gamble for twangers who want to keep their slot at Lilith Fair. "I don't understand why so many country acts, as they become more popular, take fewer chances—they don't want to mess with the style that got them famous," said banjo player Robison. "We're all about messing with styles." And oh, what a wonderful mess they've made.

Edward Norton

When Edward Norton kept us guessing as an altar boy accused of murder in *Primal Fear*, it was the first time the unknown held national audiences in the palm of his hand. It wouldn't be the last. His work in *Fear* earned him an Oscar nod and a slew of plum roles. Since then, his career has been nothing if not unpredictable. He's shown us his appetite for the controversial with risky turns as a neo-Nazi in *American History X* (for which he received a Best Actor nomination) and a disgruntled office drone in *Fight Club*. With this bloody résumé in hand, Norton, 30, then revealed his sweet tooth in his directorial debut, the romantic comedy *Keeping the Faith*. "I don't want people to know that much about me, because it will distract them from the parts I play," he once said. Don't worry, Ed: We're not even close to figuring you out.

Matt Damon

Matt Damon isn't a tormented blue-collar savant, but he plays one in the movies. Actually, he's played two: *Good Will Hunting*'s genius janitor and *The Talented Mr. Ripley*'s titular sociopath. Both are edgy, scrappy underdogs, the sort of characters it would be unwise—even unsafe—to underestimate. The same might be said of Damon himself. His broad, genial features and wraparound smile belie a fierce and restless dedication to excellence that has kept the 30-year-old on the road for over four years, leaping from one prestige project to the next. The results have been impressive: critical accolades, an Oscar for *Hunting*'s screenplay, and coveted roles in films from the likes of Robert Redford (the upcoming *The Legend of Bagger Vance*) and Billy Bob Thornton (this fall's *All the Pretty Horses*). Not bad for a college dropout who once claimed he hasn't "had any downtime to process what's going on, and where I am." Note to Damon: What's going on is you're a total smash; where you are is on top.

The End